Hagrave Jennings

Phallic Miscellanies

facts and phases of ancient and modern sex worship - as illustrated chiefly

in the religions of India

Hagrave Jennings

Phallic Miscellanies

facts and phases of ancient and modern sex worship - as illustrated chiefly in the religions of India

ISBN/EAN: 9783337262686

Printed in Europe, USA, Canada, Australia, Japan

Cover: Foto ©Andreas Hilbeck / pixelio.de

More available books at **www.hansebooks.com**

Phallic Miscellanies.

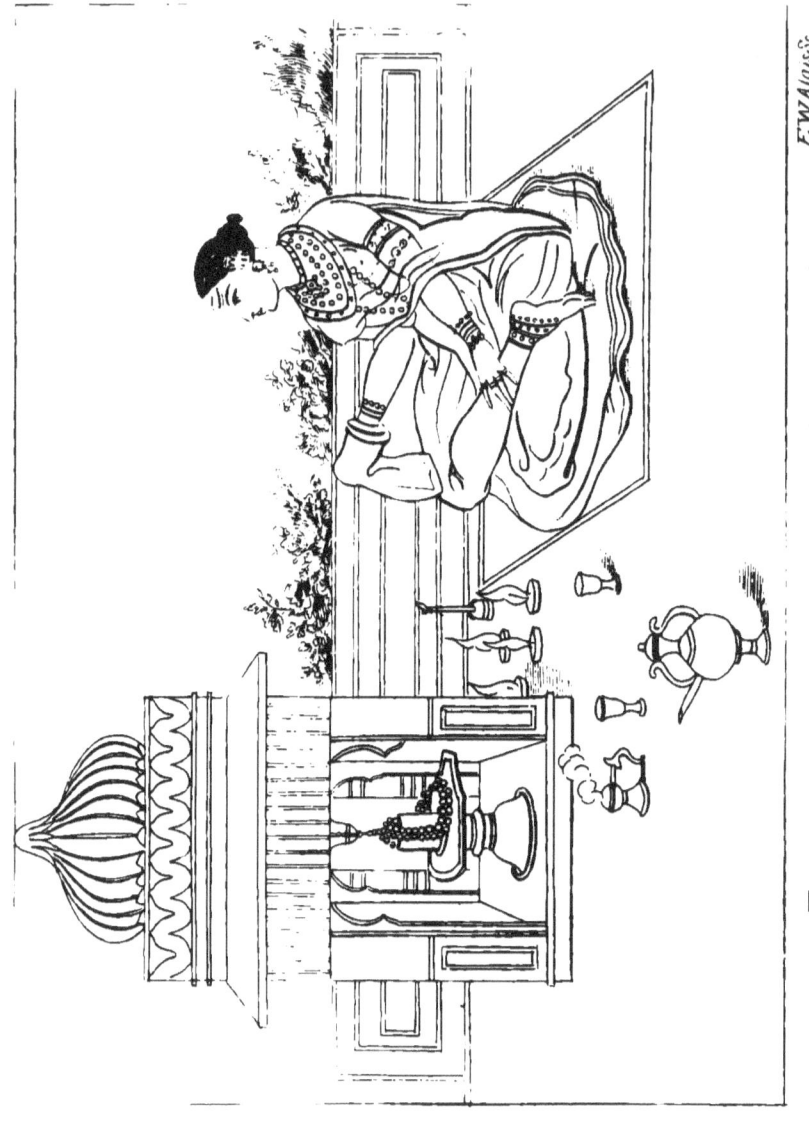

Female at the ceremony of Linga Puja.

PHALLIC MISCELLANIES;

Facts and Phases of Ancient and Modern

SEX WORSHIP,

As Illustrated Chiefly in the

Religions of India,

AN APPENDIX OF

ADDITIONAL AND EXPLANATORY MATTER

TO THE VOLUMES

Phallism and Nature Worship.

BY THE AUTHOR OF "PHALLICISM."

PRIVATELY PRINTED.

MDCCCXCI.

PREFACE.

ALL that it is necessary to say by way of preface to this book is, that, having in various former volumes, entitled severally Phallism, Nature Worship, Phallic Objects, &c., entered at some length into a consideration of the peculiarities indicated by these denominations, we now propose laying before our readers an additional mass of important matter which illustrates and throws further light upon the subject. This has been sought out with great labour and research amongst the most trustworthy sources of information, and will form a valuable appendix to the several volumes in question.

CONTENTS.

CHAPTER I. . . . . PAGE 1

India, the home of Phallic-worship—Linga described—The bull Nandi—Linga-puja—Large and small lingams—Antiquity of Linga-puja—Growth of the Hindu Pantheon—Siva the destroyer—Sacred bulls—Shrine of Ek Linga—Legend relating to rivers—The Churning of the sea—Variety of forms of Siva—Deities of India—Origin of the Universe—Hindu Triad—Aum and O'M—Jupiter Genitor—Attributes of Siva—Worship of Osiris—Identity of Egyptian, Grecian and Indian deities—Hindu temples—Ceremonies.

CHAPTER II. . . . . PAGE 20

Hindu evidence respecting the origin of Phallic worship—Legend of the wounded Hara—The four sects of worshippers instituted by Brahma—Resumption of the Lingam by Siva—Siva and Parvati propitiated—Visit of Bhrigu to Siva—The Lainga Puran on the Origin of Lingam worship—Abolition of worship of Brahma—Moral character of Hindu worship—Profligate sects—Egyptian phallus—Bacchus—Testimony of Tertullian and Clement of Alexandria—Dionysus—Directions for worship—Unsatisfactory legends—Legend of Bhima—The fourth avatar of Vishnu—Visit of Captain Mackenzie to the Pagoda at Perwuttum.

CHAPTER III. . . . . PAGE 37

Representations of Siva—Siva's quarrel with his father-in-law—Quarrel between Brahma and Vishnu—Misconduct of Siva—Bengal temples of Siva—Ancient linga idols—Siege of Somnath—Ferishtah's history—The twelve great lingams—Account of the Viri-Sawas—The Jangamas—Legend of Ravuna.

CHAPTER IV. . . . . PAGE 54
    Lingam Worship in the Sheeve Pouran.

CHAPTER V. . . . . PAGE 59
    The four kinds of stone lingas—Siva under a form called Muhakalu—Temporary images of Siva—Siva's wives—Siva's and Parvati's quarrels—Siva and Doorga—Siva's names—The heavens of Siva—Latsami—Power of the priests—Tamil poetry—Indecent worship—Dancing girls at religious ceremonies—Christian and Pagan idolatry—Religious prostitution—Worship of the female—Development of indecent practices—Sakti-puja.

CHAPTER VI. . . . . PAGE 78
    Further account of Right-hand and Left-hand worship—The practices of the Vamis or Vamacharis—The rite of Mantra Sadhana—Ceremony of Sri-Chakra—Claims of the priests to supernatural power—Legends.

CHAPTER VII. . . . . PAGE 88
    Considerations respecting the origin of Phallic worship—Comparisons between Indian and Egyptian practices and doctrines.

CHAPTER VIII. . . . . PAGE 94
    Vocabulary of words of Indian and Sanscrit origin.

PHALLIC MISCELLANIES.

CHAPTER I.

India, the home of Phallic Worship—Linga described—The Bull Nandi—Linga-puja—Large and small Lingas—Antiquity of Linga-puja—Growth of the Hindu Pantheon—Siva, the Destroyer—Sacred Bulls—Shrine of Ek-Linga—Legend relating to rivers—The Churning of the sea—Variety of Forms of Siva—Deities of India—Origin of the Universe—Hindu Triad—Aum and O'M.—Jupitor Genitor—Attributes of Siva—Worship of Osiris—Identity of Egyptian, Grecian, and Indian deities—Hindoo Temples—Ceremonies.

INDIA, beyond all other countries on the face of the earth, is pre-eminently the home of the worship of the Phallus—the Linga puja; it has been so for ages and remains so still. This adoration is said to be be one of the chief, if not the leading dogma of the Hindu religion, and there is scarcely a temple throughout the land which has not its Lingam, in many instances this symbol being the only form under which the deity of the sanctuary is worshipped.

Generally speaking, the Linga may be described as a smooth, round, black stone, apparently rising out of another stone, formed like an elongated saucer, though in reality sculptured from one block of basalt. The outline of this saucer-like stone, similar in form to what is called a jew's harp, is called Argha or Yoni: the upright stone, the type of the virile organ, is the Linga. The whole thing bears the name of Lingioni. This representation of the union of the sexes, typifies the divine sacti, or active energy in union, the procreative generative power seen throughout nature; the earth being the primitive pudendum or yoni, which is fecundated by the solar heat, the sun—the primeval Lingam, to whose vivifying rays, men and animals, plants and the fruits of the earth owe their being and continued existence. Thus, according to the Hindus, the Linga is God and God is the Linga; the fecundator, the generator, the creator in fact.

Lingas are of all sizes and of various forms. Sometimes they are extremely minute, being then enclosed in small silver reliquaries, and worn as amulets or charms upon the breast or arm. At other times they are several inches in height, as in the domestic examples, and often have the bull Nandi carved either at the end of the yoni or at the side of the emblem. The Hindus say that the bull will intercept the evil which is continually emitted from the female sacti. Upon the erection of a new village, in setting up the Linga, they are careful to turn the spout of the yoni towards the jungle, and not upon the houses or roads, lest ill fortune should rest upon them. These Lingams are of a much larger size than those just mentioned, being generally two or three feet in height. Early in the morning around these emblems may be seen the girls of the neighbourhood who are anxious for husbands, sprinkling them with water from the Ganges; decking them with garlands of bilwa flowers; performing the mudra, or gesticulation with the fingers, and while rubbing themselves against the emblem, reciting the prescribed incantations, and entreating the deity to make them the fruitful mother of children.

This is what is called the Linga puja. During its performance the five lamps are lighted and the bell frequently rung to frighten away the evil demons.

Still larger Lingas than any yet mentioned are found in the temples, some of them immense—as high as forty feet and measuring twenty-five feet in circumference. These large emblems are, as a rule, Lingas only, not in conjunction with the Yoni. Colonel Sykes in his "Account of the Ellora Excavations," (near Poonah, in the Bombay Presidency), speaking of the Bisma Kurm, says, "The first thing that meets the eye on entering the temple is the enormous hemispherical figure of the Ling (Lingam) at the end of the cave; it is always found on this scale in the arched Boodh excavations, and even at Tuncer, in a flat roofed cave, this emblem is forty-two feet in circumference, though its height is inconsiderable."

How long this worship of the Lingam has prevailed in India it is impossible to say; it is positively known to have existed for at least 1500 years, and it is estimated that about two thirds of all the Hindu people, perhaps eighty millions of souls, practise it. The idols are often described as conspicuous everywhere, in all parts of British India from the Himalaya to Ceylon. We are told that throughout the whole tract of the Ganges, as far as Benares, in Bengal, the temples are commonly erected in a range of six, eight, or twelve on each side of a ghat leading to the river, and that at Kalna is a circular group of 108 temples, erected by a raja of Bardwan. Each of the temples in Bengal consists of a single chamber, of a square form, surmounted by a pyramidal centre. The area of each is very small, the linga of black or white marble occupying the centre. What race brought the Lingam worship into India is not known, but it seems to have come from the basin of the Lower Indus through Rajputana, about the beginning of the Christian era. At Ujjain it was particularly celebrated about the period of the Mohammedan invasion, but probably long before, and one particular Linga was named Vinda-swerna; from Vindu, *drop*, Swerna, *gold*. At present there is a four-faced lingam, sometimes three-faced or tri-murti; and tri-lingam is said to be the source of the name Telinga and Telingana, the country extending north of Madras to Ganjam, and west to Bellary and Beder. The four-faced lingam is called the Choumurti Mahadeva, such as may be seen in the caves of Ellora, and of common occurrence in other districts; and a famous shrine of ek-linga, or the one lingam is situated in a defile about six miles north of Udaipur, and has hills towering around it on all sides.

This ek-lingam, or one phallus, is a cylindrical or conical stone; but there are others termed Scheslinga and Kot-Iswara, with a thousand or a million of phallic representations, all minutely carved on the monolithic emblem, having then much resemblance to the symbol of Bacchus whose orgies both in Egypt and Greece are the counterpart of those of the Hindu Baghes, so called from being clad in a tiger's or leopard's skin, as Bacchus had that of the panther for his covering. There is a very ancient temple to Kot-Iswara at the embouchure of the eastern arm of the Indus; and there are many to Scheslinga in the peninsula of Saurashtra. At the ancient Dholpur, now called Barolli, the shrine is dedicated to Gut-Iswara Mahadeva, with a lingam revolving in the yoni, the wonder of those who venture amongst its almost impervious and unfrequented woods to worship. It is said that very few Saiva followers of the south of India ever realize the lingam and the yoni as representations of the organs of the body, and when made to apprehend the fact they feel overpowered with shame that they should be worshipping such symbols.*

The age assigned by the above writer to this particular kind of worship falls very far short of what has been stated by others, and appears most probable. It has been asserted that its history goes

* See the Indian Cyclopædia.

back two thousand years before the Christian era—that it was then, as it is now, in full force—that it witnessed the rise, decline, and fall of the idolatry of Egypt, and of the great Western Mythology of Greece and Rome. "And when we reflect," says a modern writer, "on its antiquity, and on the fact that hitherto it has scarcely yielded in the slightest degree to the adverse influence of the Mohammedan race on the one hand, or to European dictation on the other; and that it exercises by its system of caste, a powerful control over the manners, customs, costumes, and social status of the entire Hindu community, it becomes a subject fraught with interest to every cultivated mind, and offers an affecting but curious example of the power of a hoary and terrible superstition in degrading and enslaving so large a portion of the human race." *

It can scarcely be questioned, theorise as writers may, that the origin of this worship is lost in antiquity; we seem able to trace it back to times when it was comparatively pure and simple—when it was the worship of one god only, the Brühm Atma, the "Breathing Soul," a spiritual Supreme Being. As time passed, however, the primitive simplicity disappeared, and rites and ceremonies became complicated and numerous. The spiritual worship of the Deity gave place to the worship of a representative image of him—a block of stone called Phallus or Linga, representing the procreative power discerned in Nature. Even this was comparatively simple at first, but it soon spread itself out in a variety of directions, until an extensive Pantheon was formed and an elaborate ritual and worship organised. It is computed that this Pantheon contains little short of a million gods and demi-gods.

It is more particularly with the god Siva we shall have to do in stating facts which illustrate the subject of Phallic worship, for the Lingam or Phallus was the emblem under which he was specially worshipped. It certainly does seem remarkable, as Mr. Sellon remarked, that of the host of divinities above mentioned, Siva should be the god whom the Hindus have delighted to honour. "As the Destroyer, and one who revels in cruelty and bloodshed, this terrible deity, who has not inaptly been compared to the Moloch of Scripture, of all their divinities, suggests most our idea of the devil. It may therefore, be concluded that the most exalted notion of worship among the Hindus is a service of Fear. The Brahmins say the other gods are good and benevolent, and will not hurt their creatures, but that Siva is powerful and cruel, and that it is necessary to appease him."

* Sellon.

The attribute of destruction is found visibly depicted in the drawings and temples throughout Bengal. To destroy, according to the Vedantis of India, the Susis of Persia, and many philosophers of the European schools, is only to generate and reproduce in another form : hence the god of destruction is held in India to preside over generation ; as a symbol of which he rides on a white bull.

The sacred bull, Nanda, has his altar attached to all the shrines of Iswara, as was that of Menes, or Apis to those of the Egyptian Osiris. He has occasionally his separate shrines, and there is one in the valley of Oodipoor, which has the reputation of being oracular as regards the seasons. The Bull was the steed of Iswara, and carried him to battle ; he is often represented upon it with his consort Isa, at full speed. The Bull was offered to Mithras by the Persian, and opposed as it now appears to Hindu faith, formerly bled on the altars of the Sun-god, on which not only the Buld-dan (offering of the bull) was made, but human sacrifices. We do not learn that the Egyptian priesthood presented the kindred of Apis to Osiris, but as they were not prohibited from eating beef, they may have done so. The shrine of Ek-Linga is situated in a defile about six miles north Oodipoor, the hills towering around on all sides are of the primitive formation, and their scarped summits are clustered with honeycombs. There are abundant small springs of water, which keep verdant numerous shrubs, the flowers of which are acceptable to the deity, especially the Kiner or Oleander, which grows in great luxuriance on the Aravulli. Groves of bamboo and mango were formerly common, according to tradition ; but although it is deemed sacrilege to thin the groves of Bal, the bamboo has been nearly destroyed : there are, however, still many trees sacred to the deity scattered around. It would be difficult to convey a just idea of a temple so complicated in its details. It is of the form commonly styled pagoda, and, like all the ancient temples of Siva, its sikra, or pinnacle, is pyramidal. The various orders of Hindu sacred architecture are distinguished by the form of the sikra, which is the portion springing from and surmounting the perpendicular walls of the body of the temple. The sikra of those of Siva is invariably pyramidal, and its sides vary with the base, whether square or oblong. The apex is crowned with an ornamental figure, as a sphynx, an urn, a ball, or a lion, which is called the kulkis. When the sikra is but the frustrum of a pyramid, it is often surmounted by a row of lions, as at Biolli. The fane of Ek-Linga is of white marble and of ample dimensions. Under an open vaulted temple, supported by columns, and fronting the four-faced divinity, is the brazen bull Nanda, of the natural size: it is cast, and of excellent proportions. The figure is perfect, except where the shot or hammer of an infidel invader has penetrated its flank in search of treasure. Within the quadrangle are miniature shrines, containing some of the minor divinities.*

Just here we may introduce a legend relating to Siva, which, if not of very great importance, is of some interest on account of its reported connection with one of our English rivers. The gods, after the creation, soon perceived that there were still many things wanting for the good of mankind, and more particularly on account of themselves. In their numerous wars with the giants, many of the gods being killed, they were informed by Vishnu that it was possible to procure a beverage, which would render them immortal. The task, however, was immense; for it consisted of throwing all the plants and trees of the universe, according to some, but, according to others, only those that grew on the sides of the White mountain or island, into the White sea; which was to be churned for a long time, in order to obtain the butter of immortality, or Amrit, the ambrosia of the western mythologists: and the old moon, which was already of Amrit, would serve as a leaven to predispose the whole mixture. The old moon was inert, and of little use; they wanted also intoxicating liquors to exhilarate themselves, and celestial nymphs for their own amusement. This churning took place in the Dwapar, or third age of the Manwantura of Chacshusa, which immediately preceded that of Noah. It lasted exactly twenty-nine years and five months, or 10,748 days, 12 hours, and 18 minutes. This is obviously the revolution of Saturn, which was in use amongst the inhabitants of the Isles in the Northern Ocean, who celebrated with great pomp, the entrance of that planet into Taurus, according to Plutarch.

It is declared in the Puranas, and acknowledged by everybody that this momentous transaction took place in the White Sea, called the Calas-odadhi or the caldron-like sea; from its being an inland one, and surrounded on all sides, or nearly so, by the land; from which circumstance it was compared to a pot or caldron. This sea was contiguous to the White Island on one side, for on account of its contiguity, the Amrit is said, in the Matsya-purana and others, to have been produced on, or near the White or silver mountain, called there also the mountain of Soma or Lunus. On

---

* Tod's Rajasth, vol. I., p. 515.

the other side it bordered on Suvarn-a-dwipa, or Ireland: for we are told in the Vrihat-Catha, that there was a sea town in that country, called Calas-a-puri, from its being situated on the Calas-odad'hi, or sea like a Calasa or caldron. This caldron-like, or landlocked sea, is evidently the Irish sea. Into this Calasa, according to the Varaha-purana, the gods flung all the plants, and agreed to churn it. This they did, says our author, in Varunaleyam or Varunasyabyam, the abode, abyam, or st'han of Varuna, the god of the sea. His abode, to this day, is well known, and is in the very centre of that sea. The Manx and Irish mythologists, according to Col. Valancey, call Varuna, *Mananan-Mac-Lir*, Mananan, the son of the sea: and his abode, according to them, is in the Isle of Man, or Mannin, as it is called by the Irish bards. According to Gen. Valancey, it was called also Manand, which answers to the Monœda of Ptolemy.

After the gods had fixed on the most proper time for the churning of the sea of milk, they soon perceived that it would be impossible for them to accomplish this tremendous work, without the assistance of giants. They made peace accordingly with them, under the most solemn promise of sharing with them the fruit of their joint labours. The gods in general are represented as a weak race, but full of cunning and very crafty; the giants, on the contrary, are very strong, and generally without much guile. The gods of the Goths, and of the Greeks and Romans, did not bear a much better character. Even among Christians there are old legends, in which the devil is most egregiously taken in by holy men.

Having thus settled the conditions, they all went to work, and gathered all the trees and plants, and flung them into the caldron-like sea. They then brought the mountain of Mandara with infinite labour. It is said that this mountain is in the peninsula, near the sea shore, and to the north of Madras. They placed it in the middle of the caldron-like sea, which they used for a churn, and mount Mandara as a churning staff. The serpent Vasuci served them instead of a rope, and they twisted him round mount Mandara, and the giants were allowed to lay hold of the snake by the head: his fiery breath scorched the giants, and they became black: the unfortunate reptile suffered much; he complained, but in vain. Mount Mandara began to sink; but Vishnu, assuming the shape of a tortoise, placed himself under it. In the Scanda-purana chapter of the Sanata-cumara-Sanhita, in the 75th section, we have a minute account of the churning of the White sea by

Vishnu, the gods and the giants: the latter had Bali at their head. After churning for five years the froth began to appear: and after three years more, Varuni or Sura, with her intoxicating liquors. The cow Camadhenu or Surabhi appeared after another year's labour. According to the Brahman-da-purana, she was worshipped by the gods, and both gods and giants were highly pleased when they saw her.

One year after, the elephant Airavata made his appearance; and the next year a horse with seven heads. Three months after, the Apsaras with Rambha-Devi at their head. Chandra or Lunus, came one year after; then after three years more, was produced Cala-cuta, a most subtile poison, flowing in large quantities; and then Vishnu became black. It was of a fiery colour, and began to set fire to the three worlds. Mankind, being alarmed, began to call out, Ah! Ah! The earth, in great distress, with Vishnu, waited on Siva, craving his assistance. Siva swallowed up the poison which stuck in his throat, and caused a most intolerable heat, which parched his throat and body. His throat turned blue; from which circumstance he is worshipped under the name of Nilacanteswara, or the lord with the blue throat.

Siva, after swallowing the poison, as related, went to Himalaya, where he buried himself in the snow. There are many places of worship dedicated to Siva, under that title; but the original one is in the White Island. It is very doubtful if our ancestors knew anything of this churning, and of the deadly poison produced by it, and of a deity swallowing it up. "In that case," says Major Wilford, "there was no such a place in the White Island. Yet I cannot resist the temptation; and I am inclined to believe it not altogether improbable, but that many of these idle legends originated in the west. If so, there might have been such a place; and it could not have been far from Camalo-dunum. The poison, which Siva drank up, is called in Sanscrit, Cala-cuta, or the black lump or mole, because it remained like a lump in Siva's throat, which looked like a cuta, a peak, also a lump or mole. Cala-cuta in Welh is y-duman, or the black lump or mole, and this was, according to Ptolemy, the name of a river in England, now called the Blackwater, in Essex. It might have been supposed once, that the black stinking mud of marshes and fens, and more particularly that of the mosses, so baneful to living creatures, was produced in consequence of this churning; probably the emblem used to signify some dreadful convulsion of nature in those parts. That such a thing happened in the western ocean, is attested by tradition: and such was its violence, and the dreadful consequences which attended it, that they could not but suppose that it had destroyed entirely the *Atlantis* and left nothing in its place but mud. A deity is then introduced, putting a stop to the progress of this black and poisonous substance, ready, according to the Puranas, to overwhelm, not only the White Island, but the whole world also. The serpent Midgard, being at the bottom of the sea, like Ananta, and vomiting torrents of deadly poison, and surrounding the world like Seshanaga, is the subject of several fundamental legends in the mythology of the Goths: but absolutely unknown to the Greeks and Romans. This Cala-cuta, or black lump of poison, stuck in Siva's throat, like the apple that Adam ate, and occasioned that protuberance, since called Adam's apple or bit."*

We have already stated that Siva is usually deemed the third person of the Hindu triad, that he represents the destructive energy, and that he appears in such a variety of forms, and on so many occasions, that scarcely a step can be taken in any department whatever of eastern science, art, or subject of literature, without encountering him in some of his varied characters. The whole race of Hindoos, it seems, is divided into two classes, denoting the worship of Siva, or of Vishnu; Brahma, the first or creative power, having no worshippers or temples. These two classes are also called Saiva-bakht, and Vishnu-bakht. We have also had occasion to inform our readers that destruction being used in the sense of renovation, the character of Siva is that of the renovator, or re-creator; associating him in character with Brahma, the producing or creative power. The variety of relations in which this and the other two members of the Hindu triad appear—whether they be introduced mythologically, metaphysically, or philosophically, has been exhibited as follows—all three are symbols of the sun, as he is typical of that great light, as the theologians express it, " whence all proceeded, and to which all must return."

Brahma	Power	Creation	Matter	The Past	Earth
Vishnu	Wisdom	Preservation	Space	The Present	Water
Siva	Justice	Destruction	Time	The Future	Fire

But these characters, or attributes, are not exclusively applicable to the three powers, as indicated above. They coalesce and participate, more or less in several. An attempt has been made to shew

---

* See Asiatic Researches, Vol. II.

in what degree, more particularly, they represent their material forms of earth, water, and fire, thus :—

Brahma and Siva are Fire, in which Vishnu ⎫
Vishnu and Brahma are Earth, in which Siva ⎬ does not participate, or participates but
Siva and Vishnu are Water, in which Brahma ⎭ remotely.

In his examination of the Vedas, or Indian Scriptures, Mr. Colebroke gives the following description of the deities of India :

"The deities invoked appear, upon a cursory inspection of the Veda, to be as various as the authors of the prayers addressed to them : but according to the most ancient annotations on the Indian Scriptures, these various names of persons and things, are all resolvable into different titles of three deities, and ultimately of one God. The Nig'hanti, or Glossary of the Vedas (which is the first part of the Niructu), concludes with three lists of names of deities : the first comprising such as are deemed synonymous with Fire ; the second with Air ; and the third with the Sun. In the last part of the Niructa, which entirely relates to deities, it is twice asserted that there are but three gods, 'Tisra eva Devatah.' The further inference, that these intend but one deity, is supported by many passages in the Veda ; and is very clearly and concisely stated in the beginning of the index to the Rigveda, on the authority of the Niructa, and of the Veda itself."

After citing several passages, Mr. Colebrooke continues :—"The deities are only three, whose places are the earth, the intermediate region, and heaven : [namely] Fire, Air, and the Sun. They are pronounced to be [deities] of the mysterious names severally ; and (Prajapati) the lord of creatures is [the deity] of them collectively. The syllable O'm intends every deity : it belongs to (Paramasht'hi) him who dwells in the supreme abode ; it pertains to (Brahma) the vast one ; to (Deva) god ; to (Ad'hyatma) the superintending soul. Other deities belonging to those several regions, are portions of the [three] gods ; for they are variously named and described on account of their different operations, 'but [in fact] there is only one deity, the Great Soul (Mahanatma). He is called the Sun ; for he is the soul of all beings ; [and] that is declared by the Sage. [The Sun] 'the soul of (jagat) what moves, and of (tast'hush) that which is fixed'; other deities are portions of him : and that is expressly declared by the Sage, 'The wise call Fire, Indra, Mitra, and Varuna, etc."

In the Manava Sastra or Institutes of Menu the origin of the

Universe is thus unfolded : " It existed only in the first divine idea, yet unexpanded, as if involved in darkness, imperceptible, indefinable, undiscoverable by reason, and undiscovered by revelation, as if it were wholly immersed in sleep. Then the sole self-existing power, who had existed from eternity, shone forth in person, expanding his idea and dispelling the gloom. With a thought he first created the waters, and placed in them a productive seed : this seed became an egg, in which he was himself born in the shape of Brahma, the great forefather of all spirits. The waters are called Nara, because they were the production of Nara, or the spirit of God : and since they were his first Ayana, or place of motion, he was thence named Narayana, or moving in the waters. In that egg the great Power sat inactive a whole year of the Creator : at the close of which, by his thought alone, he caused the egg to divide itself, and from its two divisions framed the world."

The name given by the Indians to their Supreme Deity, or Monad, is Brahm ; and notwithstanding the appearance of materialism in all their sacred books, the Brahmans never admit they uphold such a doctrine, but invest their deities with the highest attributes. He is represented as the Vast One, self-existing, invisible, eternal, imperceptible, the only deity, the great soul, the over-ruling soul, the soul of all beings, and of whom all other deities are but portions. To him no sacrifices were ever offered ; but he was adored in silent meditation. He triplicates himself into three persons or powers, Brahma, Vishnu, and Siva, and is designated by the word O'M or rather AUM.

This word O'M is a monosyllable of very profound import. It is supposed to be so holy and awful, like the name Jehovah of the Jews, as not to be guiltlessly pronounced, even by a priest. It must be contemplated, or recited mentally ; and it then is said to excite many efficacious aspirations. This awful monosyllable is triliteral, and perhaps therefore better written AUM, for three Sanscrit letters do in fact compose it : but in composition A and U coalesce in O. The first letter is supposed to be symbolical of Brahma, the creative power of the Deity ; the second of Vishnu, the preserver ; and the last of Siva, the destroyer or renovator. As all the inferior deities of the Hindoos are avataras or manifestation of, and resolve themselves into those three superior powers, so those superior powers resolve themselves ultimately into Brahm, or the supreme being, of whom the sun is the most perfect and glorious murti, or image. A combination of the three symbolical letters forms, therefore, a hieroglyphical representation of the union of the three powers or attributes, and a word that, if uttered, would be nearly expressed by our letters A U M, or O O M, dwelling a little on each letter. A name of Parvati, the consort of Siva, is Uma or Ooma, and it is perhaps hence derivable; as well as Omkar, one of the most sacred places of pilgrimage in India, dedicated to the worship of this mysterious union.

In the Institutes of Menu, many verses occur denoting the importance of this monosyllable, and of a text of the Veda closely connected with it, called the Gayatri. Among those verses are the following:

Chap. ii, v. 74. "A Brahman beginning and ending a lecture on the Veda, must always pronounce to himself the syllable OM: for unless the syllable OM precede, his learning will slip away from him; and unless it follow, nothing will be long retained." A commentator on this verse says, "As the leaf of the palasa is supported by a single pedicle, so is this universe upheld by the syllable OM, a symbol of the supreme Brahm."

76. "Brahma milked out as it were, from the three Vedas the letter A, the letter U, and the letter M, which form by their coalition the triliteral monosyllable, together with three mysterious words, *bhur, bhuva*, and *siver*." These words mean earth, sky, and heaven, and are called the vyahritis.

77. "From the three Vedas, also, the Lord of creatures incomprehensibly exalted, successively milked out the three measures of that ineffable text beginning with the word *tad*, and entitled Savitri or Gayatri."

78. "A priest who shall know the Veda, and shall pronounce to himself, both morning and evening, that syllable, and that holy text, preceded by the three words, shall attain the sanctity which the Veda confers."

79. "And a twice born man who shall a thousand times repeat those three (OM, the vyahritis, and the gayatri), apart from the multitude, shall be released in a month from a great offence, as a snake from his slough."

80. "The priest, the soldier, and the merchant, who shall neglect this mysterious text, and fail to perform in due season his peculiar acts of piety, shall meet with contempt among the virtuous."

81. "The great immutable words preceded by the triliteral syllable and followed by the gayatri, which consists of three measures, must be considered as the mouth or principal part of the Veda."

82. "Whoever shall repeat, day by day, for three years, with-

out negligence, that sacred text, shall hereafter approach the divine essence, move freely as air, and assume an ethereal form."

83. "The triliteral monosyllable is an emblem of the Supreme, the suppressions of the breath with a mind fixed on God are the highest devotion; but nothing is more exalted than the gayatri."

The suppression of the breath is thus performed by the priest: closing the left nostril with the two longest fingers of the right hand, he draws his breath through the right nostril; then closing that nostril likewise with his thumb, holds his breath while he meditates the text: he then raises both fingers off the left nostril, and emits the suppressed breath, having, during its suppression, repeated to himself the gayatri, the vyahritis, the triliteral monosyllable, and the sacred text of Brahm. By an ancient legislator it is said to imply the following meditation: "OM! earth! sky! heaven! mansion of the blessed! abode of truth!—*We meditate on the adorable light of the resplendent Generator which governs our intellects*: which is water, lustre, savour, immortal, faculty of thought, Brahm, earth, sky, heaven." The words in italics are very nearly the gayatri.

Chap. vi., v. 70. "Even three suppressions of breath, made according to the divine rule, accompanied by the triliteral phrase (bhurbhuvaswah), and the triliteral syllable (OM), may be considered as the highest devotion of a Brahman."

71. "For as the dross and impurities of metallic ores are consumed by fire, thus are the sinful acts of the human organ consumed by the suppression of breath, while the mystic words and the measures of the Gayatri are revolved in the mind."

The extreme importance that the Hindoos attach to the gayatri, renders it a text of more curiosity than perhaps a general reader will be able to discover in the words themselves, in either their familiar or recondite meaning. It is, like the holy monosyllable, to be mentally revolved, never articulated. It is taught, as we have seen in the preceding extracts from the Menu, to the three first classes, that is, to the Brahman, or priesthood; to the Kshetriya, or soldier; and to the Vaisya, or merchant; but not to the Sudra, or labourer, nor to individuals of the three first named classes if rendered by vicious propensities unworthy of the 'second birth,' promised in the holiness of this mysterious regeneration. Fasting, ablution, prayer, alms-giving, and other commendable acts, are necessary preliminaries and accompaniments to initiation in the mysteries of this 'ineffable text,' which is done by the Guru, or spiritual preceptor, in a reverent and secret manner. In the Vedas the text occurs several times, and translations of it by different Sanscrit scholars are given, with many particulars of it and other mysterious points in the Hindoo Pantheon. "There is no doubt," says the author of that work, "but that pious Brahmans would be very deeply shocked at hearing the gayatri defiled by unholy articulation, even if expressed in the most respectful manner; and many would be distressed at knowing the characters, sound, and meaning, to be in the possession of persons out of the pale of sanctity. A gentleman on the western side of India, unaware of the result, began once to recite it audibly in the presence of a pious Pandit : the astonished priest stopped his ears, and hastened terrified from his presence." In the frontispiece to that work, the character or symbol is given that would, if uttered, yield the sound of OM. The author says he once shewed it to a Brahman, who silently averted his face, evidently pained at what he unwillingly saw.

The Hindoo deities have vehicles assigned for the conveyance of themselves and wives. These are called vahan. The vahan of Siva is a bull, called Nandi. They have likewise peculiar symbols or attributes : those that more particularly designate Siva, his sakti, or anything connected with them are the Linga, or phallus, and the Trisula or Trident. The phallic emblem denotes his presiding over generation, reminding us of the Jupiter Genitor of western mythologists, with whom Sir William Jones identifies the Siva of the East.

"The Jupiter Marinus, or Neptune of the Romans, resembles Mahadeva (Siva) in his generative character; especially as the Hindoo god is the husband of Parvati, whose relation to the waters is evidently marked by her image being restored to them at the conclusion of the great festival, called Durgotsava. She is known to have attributes exactly similar to those of Venus Marina, whose birth from the sea-foam, and splendid rise from the couch in which she had been cradled, have offered so many charming subjects to ancient and modern artists."*

Another writer, Mr. Paterson, offers a passage descriptive of the character and attributes of Siva. "To Siva," he says, "are given three eyes, probably to denote his view of the three divisions of time; the past, the present, and the future. A crescent on his

* Asiatic Researches, vol. I.

forehead, pourtrays the measure of time by the phases of the moon; a serpent forms a necklace to denote the measure of time by years; a second necklace formed of human skulls marks the lapse and revolution of ages, and the extinction and succession of the generations of mankind. He holds a trident, to show that the great attributes are in him assembled and united; in another is a kind of rattle, shaped like an hour glass, and I am inclined to think that it was at first intended as such, since it agrees with the character of the deity; and a sand gheri is mentioned in the Sastra as a mode of measuring time. In the hieroglyphic of Maha Pralaya, or grand consummation of things, when time itself shall be no more, he is represented as trodden under foot by Mahakala, or eternity."

A writer in the Edinburgh Review for February, 1811, says:— "The most ancient worship of which any trace is left in Hindustan, is that of Osiris or Bacchus, whose Indian names are Iswara and Baghesa. In him, and in the gods of his family, or lineage, we recognise the divinities adored by the ancient Egyptians. That Osiris and Bacchus were the same divinity, is attested by the unanimous suffrage of all the writers of antiquity. But the most ancient Bacchus was not celebrated as the god of wine, a character ascribed to that divinity in later times. The Egyptians assert that Osiris conquered India; and indeed his expedition to that region is the subject of the celebrated epic poem of Nonnus. We by no means contend for the reality of these expeditions; but it is an indisputable fact that the worship of Osiris, distinguished by the same attributes and emblems, has continued in India from the earliest ages to this day, under the appellation of Iswara. This, we think, may be completely proved by a comparative survey of both, before, as patron of the vine, he assumed in Europe a new character.

"Osiris was adored in Egypt, and Bacchus in Greece, under the emblem of the Phallus. It is under the same emblem that he is still venerated in Hindustan; and Phalla is one of the names of Iswara in the dictionary of Amara Singha. The bull was sacred to him in Egypt. Plutarch assures us that several nations of Greece depict Bacchus with a bull's head; and that when he is invoked by the women of Elis they pray him to hasten to their relief on the feet of a bull. In India he is often seen mounted on a bull; hence one of his sanscrit names Vrishadwaja, signifying, whose ensign is a bull. Plutarch inform us that 'Nilum patrem ac servatorem suæ regionis, ac defluxum Osiridis nominant.' The Ganges in like manner is fabled by the Hindoos to flow from the tresses of Siva; hence another of his names, Gangadhara, the supporter of the Ganges. We conceive by the way, that Scaliger and Selden are mistaken in supposing that Siris, the Egyptian name of the Nile, is synonymous with Osiris. Siris seems to us the Sanscrit word Saras, a river in general, or *the* river, from its imputed superiority. Isis is the consort of Osiris; Isa that of Iswara, or Siva. The attributes of the goddesses might be shown to correspond as precisely as those of their lords.

"The attendants of Iswara resemble, in their frantic demeanour, the furious Bacchants of the god of Naxos. Many tribes of imaginary beings compose his train. The Pramatha, whose name denotes intoxication; and the Jacchi, from whom he derives the appellation of Jaccheo, or lord of the Jacchi, corrupted into Jacchus, by his western votaries. It is remarkable that many of the appellations by which the Greeks distinguish Bacchus, are also used by the Hindus; but instead of applying them to Baghesa himself, the latter refer them to his son, whilst both nations have their legends to account for them. Thus the Greeks name Bacchus, Dimeter, having two mothers; the Hindus call Scandha, the son of Baghesa, Divimatri, with the same signification. Pyrigenes, born from fire; and its equivalent in Sanscrit—Agnija, are respectively Greek and Indian appellatives of Bacchus and of Scandha. The title of Thriambus we are told by Diodorus, was assumed by the Greek Deity in his triumph after the conquest of India. Tryambo, in like-manner, is one of the most common appellations of the Indian Bacchus, but we are not aware of its signification.

"We believe we have done more than was requisite to prove the identity of the Egyptian, Grecian, and Indian Divinity; for our readers will remark that our proofs do not rest in this instance, on analogy of *sounds*, which may undoubtedly be fortuitous, but on that analogy, combined with the unity of the attributes denoted by those names, which it is impossible should be accidental."

There are five kinds of temples among the Hindoos, one of which is dedicated exclusively to the linga, another to Jugunnathu, and another is appropriated to the images of any of the gods or goddesses. The first of these is called by the general name of Mundiru; the second Daool, and the third Yorubangala. The names of the other two are Punchu-rutnu, and Nuvu-rutnu, in which the images of different gods and goddesses are placed, according to the wish of the owner.

The Mundiru is a double roofed building, the upper roof short and tapering. It contains only one room, in which is placed the image of the linga. It is ascended by steps. The floor is about three cubits by four. On the roof are placed three tridents. The building is of the Gothic order, as well as most of the other pyramidical temples of the Hindoos. Some of the temples of the linga contain two, three, or more rooms, arched over in the Gothic manner, with a porch in front for spectators. The rooms in which the image is not placed contain the things with which the ceremonies of worship are performed, the offerings, etc.

Some rich men as an act of merit, build one, and others, erect four, six, twelve, or more of these temples in one place. Some great landowners build a greater number, and employ Brahmins to perform the daily ceremonies. The relict of raja Tiluku-Chundru, of Burdwan, built one hundred and eight temples in one plain, and placed in them as many images of the linga, appointing eleven Brahmins, with other inferior servants, to perform the daily ceremonies before these images. She presented to these temples estates to the amount of the wages of these persons, the daily offerings, etc.

Many persons build flights of steps down the banks to the river side, for the benefit of persons coming to bathe, and very often also build a row of temples for the linga in front of these steps, two, four, or six on each side, and a roof supported by pillars immediately opposite the steps. At the present day, most of the persons who build these temples are the head-servants of Europeans, who appropriate a part of their fortunes to these acts of supposed merit. Near Serampore a rich Hindoo built twelve linga temples, and a flight of steps, and on the opposite side of the river, he built a house for his mistress, without any suspicion of the latter action spoiling the former.

Small square temples for the linga with flat roofs are erected in rows on the right and left before the houses of rich men, or before a college, or a consecrated pool of water, or before the descent to a flight of steps.

Very small temples like the Mundiru, two, three, or five cubits high only, and containing a linga about a foot in height, are to be seen at Benares.

Some persons build near the temples of the linga, a small house, open in front, for the accommodation of such persons who wish to die in sight of the river; and others build a temple, adjoining to that built for the linga, and dedicate it some other idol.

These temples of the linga are to be seen in great numbers on both sides of the Ganges, especially in the neighbourhood of Calcutta. The merit of building them near the river is greater than in the interior of the country, and if in a place of the river peculiarly sacred, the merit becomes the greater. The west side of the river is more sacred than the east.

The expense of one of these temples, if a single room, amounts to about two hundred rupees, and the wages and daily offerings to one linga amount to about three rupees per month. Some give the brahmin who officiates twelve anas, and others a rupee per month, with his food and clothes. Sometimes the offerings are given to him for his food, but in other cases they are presented to the brahmins of the village alternately, and the priest has money given him in their stead. These offerings consist of a pound of rice, a pint of milk, half an ounce of sugar, and two plantains. The quantity, however, is not prescribed, and other things are articled by some persons.

The daily ceremonies are:—In the morning the officiating brahmin, after bathing, goes into the temple and bows to Siva. He then anoints the image with clarified butter or boiled oil, after which, with water which has not been defiled by the touch of a shoodru, nor of a brahmin who has not bathed, he bathes the image by pouring water on it, and afterwards wipes it with a towel. He next grinds some white powder in water, and dipping the ends of his three fore-fingers in it, draws them across the linga, marking it as the worshippers of Siva mark their foreheads. Next he sits down before the image, and, shutting his eyes, meditates on the work he is commencing; then puts rice and doorva grass on the linga; next a flower on his own head, and then on top of the linga; then another flower on the linga; then others one by one, repeating incantations; then white powder, flowers, vilwu leaves, incense, meat-offerings, and a lamp before the linga; next some rice and a plantain; then he repeats the name of Siva, with some form of praise, and at last he prostrates himself before the image.

The ceremonies in the hands of a secular person, are discharged in a few minutes; if performed by a person who has sufficient leisure he spends an hour in them.

In the evening the officiating brahmin goes again to the temple, after washing his feet, etc., and prostrates himself at the door; then opening the door he places in the temple a lamp, and, as an evening oblation, presents to the image a little milk, some sweetmeats, fruit, etc., that is, such things as a Hindoo eats and drinks at those times when he does not eat his regular meals. The worship of the day closes with prostration to the image, when the brahmin locks the door and comes away.

At this temple on the 14th of the increase of the moon, in the month Phalgoonu, in the night, a festival in honour of Siva is kept. On this occasion the image is bathed four times, and four separate pujas performed during the night. Before the temple Siva's worshippers dance, sing, and revel all night, amidst the horrid din of their music.

The occasion of this festival is thus related in the puranas:— A bird-catcher was detained in a wilderness in a dark night, and took refuge in a vilwu tree under which was an image of the linga. By shaking the boughs of the trees the leaves and drops of dew fell upon the image, with which Siva was so pleased, that he declared, that whoever should from that time perform the worship of the linga on that night, he should do an act of unbounded merit.

CHAPTER II.

Hindu evidence respecting the origin of Phallic worship—Legend of the wounded Hara—The four sects of worshippers instituted by Brahma—Resumption of the Lingam by Siva—Siva and Parvati propitiated—Visit of Bhrigu to Siva—The Lainga Puran on the origin of Lingam worship—Abolition of worship of Brahma—Moral character of Hindu worship—Proflicate sects—Egyptian Phallus—Bacchus—Testimony of Tertullian and Clement of Alexandria—Dionysus—Directions for worship—Unsatisfactory legends—Legend of Bhima—The fourth avatar of Vishnu—Visit of Captain Mackenzie to the Pagoda at Perwuttum.

SO far as Hindu mythology is concerned, we find ample and interesting evidence respecting the origin of Phallic worship in the East, in the form of the adoration of the lingam. Thus in the Vamana Purana we are enlightened as follows:—" Then Hara, wounded by the arrows of Kama, wandered into a deep forest, named Daruvanam, where holy sages and their wives resided. The sages on beholding Shiva, saluted him with bended heads, and he, wearied, said to them,—' Give me alms.' Thus he went begging round the different hermitages; and, wherever he came, the minds of the sages' wives, on seeing him, became disturbed and agitated with the pain of love, and all commenced to follow him. But when the sages saw their holy dwellings thus deserted, they exclaimed,—' May the lingam of this man fall to the ground!' That instant the lingam of Shiva fell to the ground; and the god immediately disappeared. The lingam, then, as it fell, penetrated through the lower worlds, and increased in height until its top towered above the heavens; the earth quaked, and all things movable and immovable were agitated. On perceiving which Brahma hastened to the sea of milk, and said to Vishnu,—' Say, why does the universe thus tremble?' Hara replied,—' On account of the falling of Shiva's lingam, in consequence of the curse of the holy and divine sages.' On hearing of this most wonderful event, Brahma said,—' Let us go and behold this lingam.' The two gods then repaired to Daruvanam; and on beholding it without beginning or end, Vishnu mounted the king of birds and descended into the lower regions in order to ascertain its base; and for the purpose of discovering its top, Brahma in a lotos car ascended the heavens: but they returned from their search wearied and disappointed, and together approaching the lingam, with due reverence and praises, entreated Shiva to resume his lingam. Thus propitiated, that god appeared in his own form and said,—' If gods and men will worship my lingam, I will resume it ; but not otherwise. (In the Nagar Khand of the Skanda Puran, it is said that Shiva, afflicted for the loss of Sati, thus replied :—' O gods ! it was in consequence of the grief which I suffer in being separated from Sati that I cast away this lingam, apparently fallen through the curse of the sages ; but, had I not willed it, who is there in the three worlds that could have deprived me of it ? why then should I resume it.?')

To this proposal Vishnu, Brahma, and the gods assented ; and Brahma divided its worshippers into four sects, the principal one of those, that which simply worships Shiva under the symbol of the lingam; the second, that of Pashupati; the third, of Mahakala; and the fourth, the Kapali; and revealed from his own mouth the ordinances by which this worship was to be regulated. Brahma and the gods then departed, and Shiva, having resumed the lingam, was also leaving the spot, when he beheld Kama at a distance ; and, incensed with anger on remembering the pains which he had endured, looked at him with his world-consuming eye and reduced him to ashes." *Chapter 6.*

" The resumption of the lingam by Shiva," remarks Vans Kennedy in his researches into Hindu Mythology, " is related differently in the Shiva Puran, which account explains the reason of the particular form, under which that symbol is represented."

The Shiva Puran account says :—' On falling in consequence of the sages' curse, the lingam became like fire, and caused a conflagration wherever it penetrated ; the three worlds were distressed, and as neither gods nor sages could find rest, they hastened for protection to Brahma. Having heard them relate all that had happened, Brahma replied :—' After having committed knowingly a reprehensible act, why say that it was done unknowingly ? For who that is adverse to Shiva shall enjoy happiness, and yet when he came as a guest at noon-day you received him not with due honours. But every one shall reap the fruit of his good or bad actions, and the lingam therefore shall not cease to distress the three worlds until it is resumed by that god. Do ye, therefore, adopt such means as you think best for restoring tranquility to the universe.' The gods said,—' But, O Lord ! what means ought we to adopt ?' Brahma replied,—' Propitiate by adoration the mountain-born goddess, and she will then assume the form of the yoni and receive this lingam, by which means alone it can be rendered innocuous. Should you thus obtain her favourable assistance, then form a vessel of the eight kinds of leaves, place in it boiled rice and sacred plants; and having filled it with holy water, consecrate the whole with the proper prayers and invocations, and with this water, repeating at the same time suitable prayers, sprinkle the lingam. After, also, Parvati shall have under the form of the yoni received the lingam, do you erect and consecrate the form of a lingam in the yoni; and, by worshipping it with offerings of flowers, perfumes, and such things, by kindling lamps before it, and by singing and music, propitiate Maheshwara, and thus will the forgiveness and favour of that god be undoubtedly obtained.' Having heard these words, the gods and sages hastened to implore the protection of Shiva and the assistance of Parvati, as directed by Brahma; and these deities having been propitiated, Parvati, under the form of the yoni, received the lingam and thus appeased its consuming fire; and in commemoration of this event was instituted the worship of the lingam."

The Padma Puran ascribes the origin of the particular form under which this symbol is represented, to the effects of a curse imprecated on Shiva by Bhrigu. It is there said that, when, Bhrigu was sent to ascertain the preeminence of the three gods, on arriving at Kailasa he thus addressed Shiva's door-keeper :— "Quickly inform Shankara that I, the Brahman Bhrigu, am come to see him." But the door-keeper said,—'Stop, stop, if thou wishest to preserve thy life; for my lord cannot be approached at present, as he is engaged in amorous dalliance with Devi.' The divine sage being thus denied access, waited some time at the gate of Shiva's abode, and at length incensed with anger imprecated this curse :—' Since thou, O Shankara! hast thus treated me with contempt, in consequence of thy preferring the embraces of Parvati, your forms shall on that account become the lingam in the yoni." It is generally understood that it was in consequence of this curse, that Shiva was deprived of his lingam in the Daruvanan, and that Parvati assumed the form of the yoni in order to receive and render it innocuous.

The Lainga Puran relates the origin of the worship of the linga, differently.

Brahma, addressing the angels.—' When I sprang into existence, I beheld the mighty Narayana reposing on the abyss of waters; and, being under the influence of delusion, awakened him with my hand and thus addressed him,—' Who art thou that thus slumberest on this terrible ocean?' Hari awoke, and dispelling sleep from his lotos eyes, looked upon me, and then arising said,—' Welcome,

welcome, O Pitamaha! my dear son!' On hearing the first of gods smiling thus speak, I, confined within the bonds of the quality of impurity, replied,—'Why dost thou say my dear son? for know me to be the eternal god, the universal spirit, the creator, preserver, and destroyer of the three worlds.' But he immediately answered, —'Hear the truth, O four-faced! and learn that it is I who am the creator, the preserver, and the destroyer, how canst thou thus forget Nayarana the self existent and eternal Brahm? but thou committest no fault, for thy error proceeds from the delusion of Maya.' Hence arose between us a terrible combat amidst the waters of the deluge, when, to appease the contest and recall us to our senses, appeared a lingam blazing like a thousand suns. Bewildered by its radiant beams, Hari thus said to me, lost in amazement,—' I will proceed downwards in order to ascertain the termination of this wondrous column of fire, do thou, O Lord! proceed upwards and seek for its top.' Having thus spoken, he assumed the form of a boar, and I that of a swan, and we both prosecuted our search for four thousand years but being unable to ascertain its terminations, we then returned back wearied and disappointed. Thus still under the influence of delusion, we prostrated ourselves before the lingam, and were reflecting on what it could be, when we heard a voice, saying, *om, om, om,*—and shortly after appeared Shiva in the midst of that column of fire." In commemoration of this event, therefore, was the worship of the lingam instituted.

The Skande Puran relates that the abolition of the worship of Brahma is at the present day generally attributed to the inevitable consequences resulting from the curse of Shiva.

"The lingam of Shiva, having in Daruvanam fallen on the ground in consequence of the curse of the holy sages, instantly increased in size, until its base went far beyond the lowest profound, and its head towered above the heavens; and Brahma, Vishnu, Indra, and all the gods, having hastened to behold this wonder, thus spoke to one another :—" What can be its length and breath? Where can be situated its top and base?" Having thus considered, the gods said, —' O Vishnu! do thou ascertain the base of this lingam, and O Lotos-born, do thou discover its head, and let this be the place where you shall return to relate what you may have seen.' Having heard these words, Vishnu proceeded to Tartarus, and Brahma to heaven ; but high as he ascended, Pitamaha could not perceive the head of that lingam, and he was therefore returning and had arrived at the top of Meru, when *Surabhi,* as he reclined under the shade of a ketaki tree, saw him and thus spoke,—'Where hast thou gone, O Brahma! whence dost thou return? Say, can I do anything for you?' Brahma smiling, replied,—'I have been sent by the gods to discover the head of this wonderful lingam which fills the three worlds, but I have not been able to reach it. What, therefore, shall I say to them when I return; for, if I falsely assert that I have seen its top, they will require witnesses to attest the truth of it? Do thou, then, with this *ketaki*, give testimony to what I shall declare.' *Surabhi* and the *ketaki* tree consented to act as Brahma desired; and he, having made this agreement, proceeded to where the angels had remained, and thus addressed them:—'O gods! I have seen the top of this lingam, which is spacious, pure, delightful, adorned with the leaves of the *ketaki*, and wonderful to behold, but without my assistance no one can see it.' On hearing these words the immortals were astonished, and Vishnu said,—'This is most surprising; for I have penetrated through all the lower worlds, and have not been able to discover its base; but most assuredly this lingam form of Mahadeva has neither beginning, nor middle, nor end; for it was through his divine will that you, O gods and holy sages! were produced, and also this universe with all that it contains, movable and immovable; and in this lingam of the lord is centred creation, preservation, and destruction.' Brahma then said,—'O Vishnu! why art thou surprised that I have seen the top, because thou hast not been able to reach the base of this lingam; but what proof dost thou require to convince thee that I have seen it?' Vishnu, smiling, replied,—'Explain, O Brahma! how thou could'st have seen the head in heaven, while I could not discover the base in Tartarus; but if this be really the case, who are the witnesses to your having seen it?' Brahma quickly replied,—'The *ketaki* and *Surabhi*; these, O ye gods! will attest that I speak the truth.' The immortals then immediately sent for them; and when they arrived, *Surabhi* and the *ketaki* declared that Brahma had actually seen the top of the lingam. At this instant a voice was heard from heaven, saying,—'Know, O Suras! that *Surabhi* and the *ketakhi* have spoken falsely, for Brahma has not seen its top.' The immortals then imprecated this curse on *Surabhi*,—'Since thou hast with thy mouth uttered a falsehood, may thy mouth be henceforth deemed impure!' and on the *ketaki*,—'Though thou smellest sweetly, mayest thou be considered unworthy to be offered to Shiva!' After the gods had ceased speaking, the voice from heaven thus cursed Brahma:—'Since thou hast childishly and with weak understanding asserted a falsehood, let no one henceforth perform worship to thee.'"

Lieutenant Colonel Vans Kennedy remarks that these are the only accounts of the origin of this worship which occur in the Puranas, but Mr. Ward in his "Account of the Writings, Religion, &c., of the Hindus," says:—"There are several stories in the Puranas respecting the origin of the lingam worship, three of which I had translated, and actually inserted in this work, leaving out as much as possible of their offensive parts; but in correcting the proofs, they appeared too gross, even when refined as much as possible, to meet the public eye." Lieutenant Kennedy alluding to this, says:—"Mr. Ward takes every opportunity of objecting indecency and obscenity to the Hindu mythology; but, after a most attentive examination of the subject, I have not been able to discover, unless calling a spade a spade be considered a sufficient ground, the slightest foundation for such an objection in either the Purans, Upa-Purans, Ramayanum, or Mahabharat; and with regard to other Sanscrit works, I agree entirely in the justness of the opinion expressed by Mr. Wilson in a note to his translation of the Magha Duta. He says:—"I have, indeed, in this place concentrated, and in part omitted, two verses of the original, as offensive to our notions of the decorum of composition, I cannot admit, however, that Hindu literature, speaking generally, is more liable to the reproach of indecency than that of Europe: nothing can be found in their serious works half so licentious as many passages in the writings of Ovid, Catullus, Propertius, and even the elegant Flaccus. To descend to modern times, Ariosto and Boccaccio amongst the Italians, Brantome, Crebillon, Voltaire, La Fontaine, and the writers of many recent philosophical novels amongst the French, furnish us with more than parallels for the most indelicate of the Hindu writers. With respect to ourselves, not to go back to the days in which '*obscenity was wit,*' we have little reason to reproach the Hindus with want of delicacy, when we find the exceptionable, though elegant, poetry of Little generally circulated and avowedly admired. We should also recollect the circumstances of Indian society, before we condemn their authors for the ungarbled expressions which we conceive to trespass upon the boundaries of decorum. *These authors write to men only, they never think of a woman as a reader.*"

Moor in his "Hindu Pantheon," bears general testimony to the perfectly decent character of Hindu worship, on the whole, whatever may take place in exceptional cases. Speaking of the sect

of naked gymnosophists, called Lingis, and the Sactas, he says:—
"In this last mentioned sect, as in most others, there is a right-handed and decent path, and a left-handed and indecent mode of worship; but the indecent worship of this sect is most grossly so, and consists of unbridled debauchery with wine and women. This profligate sect is supposed to be numerous, though unavowed. In most parts of India, if not in all, they are held in deserved detestation; and even the decent Sactas do not make public profession of their tenets, nor wear on their foreheads the marks of their sect, lest they should be suspected of belonging to the other branch of it............It is some comparative and negative praise to the Hindus, that the emblems under which they exhibit the elements and operations of nature, are not externally indecorous. Unlike the abominable realities of Egypt and Greece, we see the phallic emblem in the Hindu Pantheon without offence; and know not, until the information be extorted, that we are contemplating a symbol whose prototype is indecent. The plates of my book may be turned and examined, over and over again, and the uninformed observer will not be aware that in several of them he has viewed the typical representation of the generative organs or powers of humanity." "From the very nature, also, of this symbol," says Kennedy, "it will be evident that it was never intended to be carried in the processions consecrated to Shiva," and Abraham Roger, two hundred years ago, has in consequence correctly stated,—"Mais quand on fait la procession par les villes avec l'idole Eswara, ce qui arrive en certains temps, on ne la porte pas sous la figure de lingam, mais sous la figure d'homme: la raison est, comme le Brahmine témoignoit, pour ce que les hommes ont plus de plasir et de contentement en la veuë d'une figure humaine que dans la veuë du lingam, en laquelle figure il est dans son pagode." *

Both Herodotus and Diodorus Siculus, as noticed by Gyraldus, though speaking of the phallus, fail to explain its precise nature and form. Mr. Payne Knight in his "Symbolical Language of Ancient Art and Mythology," says:—"In Egypt and all over Asia, the mystic and symbolical worship appears to have been of immemorial antiquity. The women of the former country carried images of Osiris in their sacred processions, with a movable phallus of disproportionate magnitude, the reason for which Herodotus does not think proper to relate, because it belonged to the mystic

* La Porte Ouverte, p. 157.

religion. Diodorus Siculus, however, who lived in a more communicative age, informs us that it signified the generative attribute; and Plutarch, that the Egyptian statues of Osiris had the phallus to signify his procreative and prolific power, the extension of which through the three elements of air, earth and water, they expressed by another kind of statue, which was occasionally carried in procession, having a triple symbol of the same attribute. The Greeks usually represented the phallus alone, as a distinct symbol, the meaning of which seems to have been among the last discoveries revealed to the initiated. It was the same, in emblematical writing, as the Orphic epithet, *Pan-genetor, universal generator*, in which sense it is still employed by the Hindus." Herodotus, in allusion to the above, says :—"To Bacchus, on the eve of his feast, every Egyptian sacrifices a hog before the door of his house, which is then given back to the swineherd by whom it was furnished, and by him carried away. In other respects the festival is celebrated almost exactly as Bacchic festivals are in Greece, excepting that the Egyptians have no choral dances. They also use, instead of phalli, another invention, consisting of images a cubit high, pulled by strings, which the women carry round to the villages. A piper goes in front; and the women follow, singing hymns in honour of Bacchus. They give a religious reason for the peculiarities of the image." Payne Knight supports his statement relative to the discovery of the meaning of the symbol by a quotation from Tertullian : Concerning the Valentinians (a sect of Ophites or of Gnostics) "After many sighings of the seers, the entire scaling of the tongue (from divulging it) an image of the virile organ is revealed." This opinion, however, has been pronounced by others as extremely questionable; "but were it admitted," says Colonel Kennedy, "it seems indisputable that the phallus was always formed in such a manner as to leave no doubt with respect to the object which it represented, and that in religious processions it was always attached to a human figure. It hence appears evident that the phallus bore no similarity to the lingam, and that, though the causes which may originally have produced the worship of these objects may have been the same in Egypt and India, still the symbols adopted for their representation, and the adoration paid to them by the Egyptians and the Hindus, differed most materially."

Clement of Alexandria was most severe in his condemnation of the abominations connected with certain festivals in which the phallus occupied a conspicuous position, but as the lingam is never carried in procession, and its worship is not celebrated by bacchanalian rites, his castigation could have had no reference, or at any rate, was not applicable to the Hindus. "Extinguish the fire, O hierophant!" he said, "be ashamed of thy own torches, O torch-bearer! the light betrays thy Jacchus: permit, if thou wish them to be reverenced, thy mysteries to be concealed by night, and thy orgies to be covered with darkness; fire does not dissimulate, but exposes and punishes all that is subjected to its power. These, therefore, are the mysteries of atheistical men; atheists I call them justly, because ignorant of the true God, they unblushingly worship an infant who was torn in pieces by the Titans, and a lamenting woman, and those parts of the body which modesty forbids us to name."

"The games and phalli consecrated to Bacchus, not only corrupt manners, but are considered shameful and disgraceful by all the world."

Clement then speaks of a certain event, in commemoration of which, "was this mystery instituted, and phalli erected in every city in honour of Dionusos; so that Heraclitus even says that misfortune would ensue, if processions were not made, and hymns sung, and pudenda shamelessly worshipped, in honour of Dionusos. This then is the Hades and the Dionusos, in whose honour men become agitated with bacchanalian madness and fury; not so much, in my opinion, an account of natural inebriation, as in consequence of the reprehensible ceremonies which were first instituted in commemoration of that abominable turpitude."

The event just referred to is this:—Dionysus was particularly anxious to descend to Hades, but was ignorant of the way; a certain man named Prosymnus offered to show him the same, provided he would grant him a specified reward. "The reward," says Clement, "was a disgraceful one, though not so in the opinion of Dionysus: it was an Aphrodisian favour that was asked. The god was not reluctant to grant the request made to him, and promised to fulfil it should he return, conforming his promise with an oath. Having learned the way, he departed and again returned: he did not find Prosymnus for he had died. In order to acquit himself of his promise to his lover, he rushed to his tomb, burning with unnatural lust. Cutting a fig-branch that came to his hand, he shaped the likeness of the *membrum virile*, and sat over it; thus performing his promise to the dead man. As a mystic memorial of this incident, *phalloi* are raised aloft in honour of Dionysus through the various cities."

The character of Lingam worship may be gathered from the ritual prescribed in the Lainga Puran, which we find to be as follows: "Having bathed in the prescribed manner, enter the place of worship; and having performed three suppressions of the breath, meditate on that god who has three eyes, five heads, ten arms, and is of the colour of pure crystal, arrayed in costly garments, and adorned with all kinds of ornaments: and having thus fixed in thy mind the real form of Maheshwara, proceed to worship him with the proper prayers and hymns. First, sprinkle the place and utensils of worship with a bunch of darbha dipped in perfumed water, repeating at the same time the sacred word *Om*, and arrange all the utensils and other things required in the prescribed order; then in due manner and repeating the proper invocations, prayers and hymns, preceded by the sacred word *Om*, prepare thy offerings. For the padiam (water for the ablution of the feet), these should consist of ushiram (the root of the Andropogon muricatus), sandal, and sweet-smelling woods: for the achamanam (water for rinsing the mouth), of mace, camphor, bdellium, and agallochum, ground together; and for the arghya (a particular kind of oblation, which, consisted of different articles in the worship of different deities), of the tops of Kusha grass, prepared grains of rice, barley, sesamum, clarified butter, pieces of money, ashes and flowers. At the same time, also, must be worshipped Nandi (the principal attendant of Shiva, and supposed to be a portion of that god, who granted a son as a boon to a holy ascetic named Shilada, and also consented that he would be born as that son), and his wife, the daughter of Marut. Having then, with due rites, prepared a seat, invoke with the prescribed prayers the presence of Parameshwara, and present to him the *padiam*, *achamanam* and *arghya*. Next bathe the lingam with perfumed water, the five products of the cow, clarified butter, honey, the juice of the sugar-cane, and lastly pour over it a pot of pure water, consecrated by the requisite prayers. Having thus purified it, adorn it with clean garments and a sacrificial string, and then offer flowers, perfumes, frankincense, lamps, fruit, and different kinds of prepared eatables, and ornaments. Thus worship the lingam with the prescribed offerings, invocations, prayers and honours, and by circumambulating it, and by prostrating thyself before Shiva, represented under this symbol."

Colonel Vans Kennedy says that at the present day the whole of this ritual is not observed, nor is this worship performed in that costly manner which is recommended in the Purans. But the worship of all the deities consists of sixteen essential requisites:—1, *Asanam*, the preparing a seat for the god; 2, *Asahanam*, the invoking his presence; 3, *padiam*; 4, *achamanam*; 5, *Arghya*; 6, bathing the image; 7, clothing it; 8, investing it with a sacrificial string: offerings of; 9, perfumes; 10, flowers; 11, incense; 12, lamps; 13, naivedya, *i.e.* offerings consisting of fruits and prepared eatables; 14, betel leaf; 15, prayers, &c.; 16, circumambulation. The more of these acts that are performed the more complete is the worship; but at present it in general consists of nothing more than presenting some of the prescribed offerings, and muttering a short prayer or two while the lingam is circumambulated: the rest of the acts being performed by the officiating priest.

This worship, it seems, need not be performed at a temple, any properly purified place will do; it is most efficacious when performed on the bank of some holy river, before a lingam formed of clay, which, on the termination of the worship, is thrown into the sacred stream.

Colonel Kennedy says:—" The legends respecting the origin of the worship of the lingam, cannot satisfy the philosophical enquirer; and the real cause, therefore, which produced the adoration of so singular an object might appear to be a curious subject of speculation. But, though in the Purans there are copious descriptions of the high importance of this worship, and of the spiritual advantages to be derived from it, still these works contain not the slightest indication from which any just conclusion could be formed, with respect to either the period when it was first introduced, or the motives which may have occasioned the substitution of this symbol for the image of Shiva. Yet it seems probable that this change had not been effected at the time when the Vedas were composed, and that the earliest record of this worship which has been preserved is contained in the Purans. But, as in those sacred books there is not the least appearance of its being either mystical or symbolical, it must be evident that if it originated in such causes they have long ceased to exist; and consequently that the speculations on this subject, in which the literati of Europe have indulged, are totally incompatible with the simple principles, as far as they are known, on which this worship is founded. For, in fact, both in the Purans and by the Hindus of the present day, the lingam is held to be merely a visible type of an invisible deity; and nothing whatever belongs to its worship, or to the terms in which this is mentioned, which has the slightest tendency to lead the thoughts, from the contemplation of the god, to an undue consideration of the object by which he is typified. But it is impossible to understand by what process of reasoning the founders of the Hindu religion were induced to place Shiva among the divine hypostases; for they supposed, at the same time, that dissolution and death proceeded from the fixed laws of nature, and that his power was not called into exertion until after the termination of twelve millions of years. During the whole, therefore, of this inconceivable period, what functions could be ascribed to this god consistent with his character of destroyer? This difficulty, however, seems to have been very soon obviated by investing him with the attributes of the Supreme Being, and even in the Purans it is under this character that he is generally represented. As, therefore, the attributes which are, according to the Hindus, peculiar to the one god are immovability and inaction, Shiva is described as being principally engaged in devout meditation, and as exerting his divine power through the means either of Devi (or his energy personified) or of certain forms which he creates for the occasion, such as Bhairava and Virabhadra. In Hindu mythology, consequently, there are only three legends, the destruction of the Tripura Asuras, and of the Asuras Audhaka, and Jalandhara, in which Shiva appears as the actor, unconnected with any reference to the worship of the lingam. But on the introduction of this worship, not a lingam seems to have been erected without its foundation having been ascribed to some miraculous appearance of Shiva; and hence have originated a multiplicity of legends in the highest degree puerile, and every one erring against the just principle,—

> Nec deus intersit, nisi dignus vindice nodus
> Inciderit.

For in the Shiva Puran, Suta thus speaks: "Innumerable are the lingams which are adorned, as the type of Shiva, in heaven, earth, and Tartarus; but where some of these are erected, there Shiva for the good of the three worlds appeared, and consequently whoever visits and worships them, acquires more complete remission of sins and a greater degree of holiness. Even of these, however, the number is unascertainable, but the twelve Jyotisha lingams are considered the most sacred; there are, of course, many others, the worship of which insures the remission of sins and final blessedness."

Legend from the Shiva Puran.

A Rakshasa, named Bhima, the son of Kumbakarna, having obtained invincible might as a boon from Brahma, commenced exerting his newly acquired power by attacking the king of Kamarupa. Him he conquered, and having seized his riches and kingdom, he placed him in chains in a solitary prison. This king was eminently pious, and, notwithstanding his confinement, continued daily to make clay lingams, and to worship Shiva with all the prescribed rites and ceremonies. Meanwhile the Rakshasa continued his conquests, and everywhere abolished the religious observances and worship enjoined by the Vedas; and the immortals also, were reduced by his power to great distress. At length the gods hastened to implore the protection of Shiva, and to obtain his favour by the worship of clay lingams; and Shambu, being thus propitiated, assured them that he would effect the destruction of the Rakshasa through the medium of the king of Kamarupa, who was his devoted worshipper. At this time the king was engaged in profound meditation before a lingam, when one of the guards went and informed the Rakshasa that the king was performing some improper ceremonies in order to injure him. On hearing this, the Rakshasa, enraged, seized his sword and hastened to the king, whom he thus addressed:—"Speak the truth, and tell me who it is that thou worshippest, and I will not slay thee, but otherwise I will instantly put thee to death." The king having considered, placed his firm reliance in the protection of Shiva, and replied undauntedly,—"In truth, I worship Shankara: do thou what thou pleasest." The Rakshasa said,—"What can Shankara do to me? for I know him well, and that he once was obliged to become the servant of my uncle (Ravana); and thou, trusting in his power, did'st endeavour to conquer me, but defeat was the consequence. Until, however, thou showest me thy lord, and convincest me of his might, I shall not believe in his divinity." The king replied, —"Vile as I am, what power have I over that god? but mighty as he is, I know that he will never forsake me." Then Rakshasa said,—"How can that delighter in ganja (an intoxicating drug prepared from the hemp plant) and inebriation, that wandering mendicant, protect his worshippers? let but thy lord appear, and I will immediately engage in battle with him!" Having thus spoken, he ordered the attendance of his army, and then, revisiting the king, the mighty Rakshasa, while he smote the lingam with his sword, thus, laughing, said,—"Now behold the power of thy lord." But scarce had the sword touched the lingam than Hara instantly issued from it, exclaiming,—" Behold! I am Ishwara, who appears for the protection of his worshipper, on whom he always bestows safety and happiness; and now learn to dread my might." On hearing this spoken, Shiva engaged in combat with the Rakshasa, and after fighting with him for some time, at length with the fire of his third eye reduced him and all his army to ashes; and in commemoration of this event was the spot where it occurred rendered sacred, and the lingam, under the name of Bhimashankara, an object of pilgrimage and worship until all succeeding ages. (*From the legend Jyotisha-linga Mahatmyam*).

Colonel Kennedy says :—" On perusing this legend, it will immediately occur that it is a mere imitation of the fourth avatar of Vishnu, the concluding part of the account of which is thus given in the Padma Puran :—' Hiranyakashipu having ordered his son Pralhada to be put to death on account of his devotion to Vishnu, and all means employed for this purpose having proved ineffectual, the king of the Daityas was astonished, and with gentleness addressed his son :—' Where is that Vishnu whose pre-eminence thou hast declared before me, and who, as thou sayest, was called Vishnu because he pervades all things, and consequently, being omnipresent, he must also be the Supreme Being? Show to me a proof of the divine power and qualities which thou ascribest to him, and I will acknowledge the divinity of Vishnu; or let him conquer in battle me, who have obtained the boon of being unslayable by any existing thing.' Pralhada astonished, replied,—' Narayana, the eternal, omnipotent, omnipresent, and Supreme Spirit dwells in heaven, and man cannot obtain the view of his divine form through anger and hatred, but, though unseen, he is present in all things.' Having heard these words, Hiranyakashipu was incensed with anger, and, reviling his son, said,—' Why dost thou thus with endless boasts exalt the power of Vishnu?' and then striking a pillar of his royal hall, thus continued : If Vishnu pervades all things let him appear in this pillar, or I will this moment put thee to death.' This said, he struck the pillar with his sword, and instantly from it burst a loud and dreadful sound, while Vishnu issued forth under a fearful form, half man and half lion."

" But as the avatars of Vishnu are unquestionably an essential part of the Hindu religion, since they are noticed in the Vedas, Upanishads, and Purans, and as the miraculous appearances of Shiva, on which the sanctity of various lingams is founded, are not generally acknowledged by the Hindus, and are mentioned only in the Shanka and Shiva Purans, it must necessarily follow that the fourth avatar of Vishnu is the original from which the above legend of Bhima Shankara has been merely copied. The introduction, however, of a new mode of worship, is always, as experience has shewn, supported by miracles; and it may therefore be concluded that the legends respecting the Jyolisha lingams, at least, are as ancient as the first institution of the worship of the lingam. In which case it will be evident that the transferring by the Shaivas to Shiva of the peculiar attribute of Vishnu, that of preservation, and their founding various miracles on such transfer, are convincing proofs that Vishnuism must have existed before the present form of Shivaism; and that, in inventing these miracles, the Shaivas have wished to ascribe to the god of their particular adoration similar manifestations of divine power to those by which Vishnu was supposed to be peculiarly distinguished." *

An account was published, about a hundred years ago, by Captain Colin Mackenzie, of a visit he had lately paid to the Pagoda at Perwuttum, the home of the Linga Mallikarjuna or Sri Saila. He said;—" Having sent notice to the manager of the revenues, that I was desirous of seeing the padoga, provided there was no objection, I was informed at noon, that I might go in. On entering the fourth gate, we descended by steps, and through a small door, to the inner court, where the temples are: in the centre was the pagoda of Mallecarjee, the principal deity worshipped here. From hence I was conducted to the smaller and more ancient temple of Mallecarjee, where he is adored, in the figure of a rude stone, which I could just distinguish, through the dark vista of the front building on pillars. Behind this building, an immense fig tree covers with its shade the devotees and attendants, who repose on seats, placed round its trunk, and carpeted. Among these, was one Byraggy, who had devoted himself to a perpetual residence here; his sole subsistence was the milk of a cow, which I saw him driving before him: an orange coloured rag was tied round his loins, and his naked body was besmeared with ashes.

" The weather being warm, I was desirous of getting over as much of this bad road, as I could, before noon : my tents and baggage had been sent off at four A.M., and I only remained near the pagoda with the intention of making some remarks on the sculptures of its wall, as soon as daylight appeared.

* Vans Kennedy, Hindu Mythology.

"But the Brahmins, with the Rajpoot amuldar (who had hitherto shewn a shyness that I had not experienced in any other part of the journey), came to request, that as I was the first European who had ever come so far to visit Mallecarjee, and had been prevented from seeing the object of their worship, by yesterday not being a lucky day, I would remain with them that day, assuring me that the doors would be opened at ten o'clock. I agreed to wait to that hour, being particularly desirous of seeing by what means the light was reflected into the temple, which the unskilfulness of my interpreter could not explain intelligibly to my comprehension. Notice being at last given, at about half-past eight, that the sun was high enough, the doors on the east side, the gilt pagoda were thrown open, and a mirror or reflecting speculum was brought from the Rajpoot amuldar's house. It was round, about two feet in diameter, and fixed to a brass handle, ornamented with figures of cows; the polished side was convex, but so foul, that it could not reflect the sunbeams; another was therefore brought, rather smaller, and concave, surrounded by a narrow rim, and without a handle. Directly opposite to the gate of the pagoda is a stone building, raised on pillars, enclosing a well, and ending in a point; and being at the distance of twelve or fourteen feet, darkens the gateway by its shadow, until the sun rises above it: this no doubt has been contrived on purpose to raise the expectation of the people, and by rendering the sight of the idol more rare, to favour the imposition of the Brahmins. The moment being come, I was permitted to stand on the steps in front of the threshold without (having put off my shoes, to please the directors of the ceremony, though it would not have been insisted on), while a crowd surrounded me, impatient to obtain a glimpse of the awful figure within. A boy being placed near the doorway, waved and played the concave mirror in such a manner, as to throw gleams of light into the pagoda, in the deepest recess whereof was discovered by means of these coruscations, a small, oblong, roundish white stone with dark rings, fixed in a silver case. I was permitted to go no further, but my curiosity was now sufficiently satisfied. It appears, that this god Mallecarjee, is no other than the Lingam, to which such reverence is paid by certain castes of the Gentoos; and the reason why he is here represented by stones unwrought, may be understood from the Brahmin's account of the origin of this place of worship. My interpreter had been admitted the day before into the sanctum sanctorum, and allowed to touch the stone, which he says is smooth and shining, and that the dark rings or streaks, are painted on it; probably it is an agate, or some other stone of a similar kind, found near some parts of the Kistna, and of an uncommon size.

"The Brahmins gave me the following account of the origin of the pagoda. At Chundra-gumpty-patnum, twelve parvus down the river, on the north side, formerly ruled a Raja, of great power; who being absent several years from his house, in consequence of his important pursuits abroad; on his return, fell in love with his own daughter, who had grown up during his long absence. In vain the mother represented the impiety of his passion; proceeding to force, his daughter fled to these deserts of Perwuttum, first uttering curses and imprecations against her father; in consequence of which, his power and wealth declined, his city, now a deserted ruin, remains a monument of divine wrath, and himself, struck by the vengeance of heaven, lies deep beneath the waters of Puttela-gunga, which are tinged green by the string of emeralds that adorned his neck.

"The princess was called Mallicadivi, and lived in this wilderness. Among her cattle, was a remarkably fine black cow, which, she complained to her herdsman, never gave her milk. He watched behind the trees, and saw the cow daily milked by an unknown person; Mallicadivi informed of this, placed herself in a convenient situation, and beholding the same unknown person milking the cow, ran to strike him with the iron rod, or mace, which she held in her hand; but, the figure suddenly disappeared, and to her astonishment, nothing remained but a rude shapeless stone. At night, the god appeared to her in a dream, and informed her, he was the person that milked the cow; she therefore, on this spot, built the first temple that was consecrated to the worship of this deity, represented by a rude stone. This is the second temple that was shewn yesterday, where he is exhibited in the rude state of the first discovery, and is called Mudi-Nulla-carjee or Mallacarjee; the other temples were afterwards built, in later times, by Rajahs and other opulent persons. The Lingam shewn by reflected light in the gilded temple, has also its history, and stories, still more absurd and wonderful, attached to it. It was brought from the city of Chundra-goompty-patnam. The princess, now worshipped as a goddess, is also called Brama-Rumbo or Strichillumrumbo, from which the pagoda is sometimes called Strichillum.

CHAPTER III.

Representations of Siva—Siva's quarrel with his father-in-law—Quarrel between Brahma and Vishnu—Misconduct of Siva—Bengal temples of Siva—Ancient linga idols—Siege of Somnath—Ferishtah's history—The twelve great lingams—Account of the Viri-Saivas—The Jangamas—Legend of Ravunu.

SIVA, has the second place among the Hindoo deities, though in general, in allusion to their offices, the principal gods are classed thus: Brahma, Vishnu, Siva. Siva, personifies destruction or reproduction, for Hindu philosophy excludes, while time shall exist, the idea of complete annihilation: to destroy is, therefore, but to *change*, or *recreate*, or *reproduce*.

This god is represented in various ways. In the dhyanu he appears as a white or silver coloured man with five faces; an additional eye (one of his names is Trilochunu, the three eyed), and a half-moon on each forehead; four arms; in the first a purushao; in the second a deer; with the third giving a blessing, and with the fourth forbidding fear; sitting on a water-lily, and wearing a tiger's skin. He is worshipped in the daily puja of the brahmins, who silently meditate upon him in this form.

At other times Siva is represented with one head, three eyes, and two arms, riding on a bull, covered with ashes, naked, his eyes inflamed with intoxicating herbs, having in one hand a horn, and in the other a musical instrument called a dumbooru.

Another of his images is the linga, a smooth black stone very much like a sugar-loaf in shape, with a projection of a spoon shape.

There are three different stories respecting the origin of this image. The Purana called Doorga-bhagavata gives the following account: King Dukshu, having had a quarrel with Siva, refused to invite him to a sacrifice which he was performing. Siva had married Sutee, the daughter of Dukshu. She resolved, uninvited, to attend at this sacrifice; but while there, she was so overcome by the abuse which Dukshu poured upon her husband, that she died.

The ground of the quarrel between Siva and his father-in-law was this: It was the custom for the junior branches of a family, as they arrived at an assembly, to bow to their older relation. On a certain occasion Siva neglected, or refused, to bow to his father-in-law, who began to abuse him in such a manner that a dreadful enmity was raised which ended in the destruction of Dukshu.

On hearing the news of the fate of his beloved wife, Siva, in vexation, renounced a secular life, and assumed the profession of a religious mendicant called a sunyasee. As a naked sunyasee he wandered from forest to forest, in the bitterness of grief. At length he arrived in a certain wilderness were many moonees were performing religious austerities, by the side of the river at a distance from their homes. The wives of these moonees, on beholding this naked, dirty, and withered sunyasee, asked him who he was, and why he was wandering up and down in this state? He related to them the cause of his sorrow, viz., that he had been deprived of his wife, and was overwhelmed with distress on her account. The women laughed at him, and pretended to doubt his relation, declaring that his body was so withered, that all desires must have been extinguished. In this manner they provoked Siva, till at length he seized the wife of one of the moonees and deflowered her. The moonee on hearing this relation, pronounced a curse on Siva, and he became an hermaphrodite. As soon as the curse had taken effect, the linga sunk into patalŭ, the world of serpents, and ascended into the boundless space.

Before this period, a fierce quarrel had taken place betwixt Brahma and Vishnu, as to which of them was the greatest, the former as the creator, or the latter as the preserver or cherisher, of all. They appealed to Siva, who left it to be determined by a trial of strength at some future time, when he should have leisure.

Siva at length proposed to the two gods to settle their quarrel in this way: one of them should ascend, and endeavour to ascertain the height of the linga, and the other descend, and bring up word of its depth. Brahma ascended, and Vishnu plunged into patalŭ. In this way both the gods tried their utmost efforts, but could not find either the height or the depth of the linga. As Brahma ascended, he met a flower which had fallen from the top of the linga, and asked how far it was to the top. The flower told him that it had been falling from the head of the linga so many kŭlpŭs (one kŭlpŭ is four hundred and thirty-two millions of years of mortals) and had not reached the earth yet; what hope was there then of his reaching the top? Brahma related the account of the difference betwixt him and Vishnu, and that upon this trial of their powers the point of pre-eminence was to be decided. The flower advised Brahma to tell the assembled gods, that he had gone to the top, and if they doubted the fact, he might call him to confirm it.

Brahma descended, and Vishnu came up disappointed in his attempt to get to the bottom of the linga. When the two gods arrived in the assembly, Brahma declared that he had been to the top, and brought the flower to prove it. Vishnu confessed his disappointment, and charged the flower with witnessing a falsehood. To this all the gods assented, and Vishnu pronounced a curse upon the flower, that it should never be received among the offerings presented to Siva.

After the matter was thus disposed of, the gods resolved that the worship of the linga should have the precedency of every other worship; that the benefits attending its worship should be boundless, and that the heaviest curses should fall on those who neglected to worship this image. So much for the account in the Doorga-bhagavata: in the Kaduru-khundu the origin of the worship is thus mentioned:

When the gods resolved to churn the sea, in order to obtain the water of life, become immortal, and overcome the usoorus, they were greatly afraid lest the usoorus should seize the water of life, and become immortal also. When the water of life came up, they contrived to send the usoorus to bathe; but after bathing, they arrived before the gods had drank the life-giving beverage. To draw off their attention, Vishnu assumed the form of a most beautiful female. This contrivance was successful.

The god Siva hearing that Vishnu had assumed this form, went to the spot, and was so overcome by the charms of Mohinee, that he was about to seize her by force: she fled, and Siva followed her; mad with lust, he pursued her till she could run no longer, when she turned, and pronouncing a curse upon him by which he became a hermaphrodite, she immediately assumed her original form, viz., that of Vishnu. Siva was so enraged, that all the gods, full of fear, arrived to soften him by praise. He at length consented to dismiss his anger on condition that the linga should become an object of universal worship.

Another account of the origin of this worship is contained in some of the other puranas: At the time of a universal destruction of the world all the gods are absorbed in what is called akashu; the linga alone remains. The puranas, therefore, say that as all the gods except the linga are absorbed in the akashu, he who worships the linga, obtains the unbounded merit of embracing all the deities at once. From these stories, temples innumerable have arisen in India, and a Siva linga placed in each of them, and worshipped as a god.

The worship of Siva under the type of the Linga, is almost the only form in which that deity is reverenced. Its prevalence throughout the whole tract of the Ganges, as far as Benares, is sufficiently conspicuous. In Bengal the temples are commonly erected in a range of six, eight, or twelve, on each side of a Ghat, leading to the river. At Kalna is a circular group of one hundred and eight temples, erected by the Rajah of Bardwan. Each of the temples in Bengal consists of a single chamber, of a square form, surmounted by a pyramidal centre; the area of each is very small, the Linga, of black or white marble, occupies the centre; the offerings are presented at the threshold. Benares, however, is the peculiar seat of this form of worship: the principal deity, Visweswara, is a Linga, and most of the chief objects of the pilgrimage are similar blocks of stone. Particular divisions of the pilgrimage direct visiting forty-seven Lingas, all of pre-eminent sanctity; but there are hundreds of inferior note still worshipped, and thousands whose fame and fashion have died away. If we may believe Siva, indeed, he counted a hundred Pararrdhyas in the Kasi, of which, at the time he is supposed to tell this to Devi, he adds sixty crore, or six hundred millions were covered by the waters of the Ganges A Pararrdhya is said, by the commentator on the Kasi-Khanda, in which this dialogue occurs, to contain as many years of mortals as are equal to fifty of Brahma's years.

This worship of Siva, under the type of the Linga, is also, perhaps, the most ancient object of homage adopted in India, subsequently to the ritual of the Vedas, which was chiefly, if not wholly, addressed to the elements, and particularly to Fire. How far the worship of the Linga is authorised by the Vedas, is doubtful, but it is the main purport of several of the Puranas—such as the Skanda-Purana, the Siva, Brahmanda, and Linga Puranas. There can be no doubt of its universality at the period of the Mohammedan invasion of India. The idol destroyed by Mahmud of Ghizni, was nothing more than a Linga, being, according to Mirkhond, a block of stone of four or five cubits long, and of proportionate thickness. The passage from the *Rozet as Sefa* (cited in the Asiatic Researches, vol. 17), runs thus :—"The temple in which the idol of Somnath stood, was of considerable extent, both in length and breath, and the roof was supported by fifty-six pillars in rows. The idol was of polished stone, its height was about five cubits, and its thickness in proportion : two cubits were below ground. Mahmud having entered the temple, broke the stone Somnath with a heavy mace; some of the fragments he ordered to be conveyed to Ghizni, and they were placed at the threshold of the great Mosque."

PHALLIC MISCELLANIES.

Another authority, the Tebkat Akbeeri, a history of Akber's reign, with a preliminary Sketch of Indian History, has the following: "In the year 415 (Hijera) Mahmud determined to lead an army against Somnath, a city of the seashore, with a temple appertaining to the followers of Brahma; the temple contained many idols, the principal of which was named Somnath. It is related in some histories that this idol was carried from the Kaaba, upon the coming of the Prophet, and transported to India. The Brahminical records, however, refer it to the times of Krishna, or an antiquity of 4000 years. Krishna, himself, is said to have disappeared at this place.

When the Sultan arrived at Neherwaleh (the capital of Guzerat) he found the city deserted, and carrying off such provisions as could be procured, he advanced to Somnath: the inhabitants of this place shut their gates against him, but it was soon carried by the irresistable valour of his troops, and a terrible slaughter of its defenders ensued. The temple was levelled with the ground: the idol Somnath, which was of stone, was broken to pieces, and in commemoration of the victory, a fragment was sent to Ghizni, where it was laid at the threshold of the principal mosque, and was there many years.

Ferishtah, the historian, supplies a much more graphic, if not reliable account. He says: "When the garrison of Sumnat beheld their defeat, they were struck with confusion and fear. They withdrew their hands from the sight, and issuing out at a gate towards the sea, to the number of four thousand embarked in boats, intending to proceed to the island of Sirindiep. But they did not escape the eyes of the king. He seized upon boats which were left in a neighbouring creek, and manning them with rowers and some of his best troops, pursued the enemy, taking and sinking some of their boats while others escaped. Having then placed guards round the walls and at the gates, he entered Sumnat, with his son and a few of his nobles and principal attendants. When they advanced to the temple, they saw a great and antique structure, built of stone, within a spacious court. They immediately entered it, and discovered a great square hall, having its lofty roof supported by fifty-six pillars, curiously turned and set with precious stones. In the centre of the hall stood Sumnat, an idol of stone, five yards in height, two of which were sunk in the ground.

"The king was enraged when he saw this idol, and raising his mace, struck off the nose from the face. He then ordered that two pieces of the image should be broken off, to be sent to Ghizni, there to be thrown at the threshold of the public mosque, and in the court of his palace. Two more fragments he reserved to be sent to Mecca and Medina. When Mahmood was thus employed in breaking up Sumnat, a crowd of Brahmins petitioned his attendants, and offered some crores (ten millions) in gold, if the king should be pleased to proceed no further. The Omrahs endeavoured to persuade Mahmood to accept the money; for they said that breaking up the idol could not remove idolatry from the walls of Sumnat, that therefore it would serve no purpose to destroy the image, but that such a sum of money given in charity, among believers, would be a very meritorious action. The king acknowledged that what they said was, in some measure, true; but should he consent to that bargain, he might justly be called a seller of idols; and that he looked upon a breaker of them as a more honourable title. He therefore ordered them to proceed. The next blow having broken up the belly of Sumnat, which had been made hollow, they discovered that it was full of diamonds, rubies, and pearls, of a much greater value than the amount of what the Brahmins had offered, so that a zeal for religion was not the sole cause of their application to Mahmood."

It is said, by some writers, that the name of this idol is a compound word of Sum and Nat; Sum being the name of the prince who erected it, and Nat the true name of the god; which in the language of the Brahmins, signifies Creator. In the time of eclipses we are told that there used to be forty or fifty thousand worshippers at this temple; and that the different princes of Hindostan had bestowed, in all, two thousand villages, with their territories, for the maintenance of its priests; besides the innumerable presents received from all parts of the empire. It was a custom among these idolaters, to wash Sumnat, every morning and evening, with fresh water from the Ganges, though that river is above one thousand miles distant.

Among the spoils of this temple was a chain of gold, weighing forty maunds, which hung from the top of the building by a ring. It supported a great bell, which warned the people to the worship of the god. Besides two thousands Brahmins, who officiated as priests, there belonged to the temple five hundred dancing-girls, three hundred musicians, and three hundred barbers, to shave the devotees before they were admitted to the presence of Sumnat. The dancing-girls were either remarkable for their beauty or their quality, the Rajas thinking it a honour to have their daughters admitted. The king of Ghizni found in this temple, a greater quantity of jewels and gold, than, it is thought, any royal treasury contained before. In the history of Eben Assur, it is related that there was no light in the temple, but one pendant lamp, which being reflected from the jewels, spread a strong and refulgent light over the whole place. Besides the great idol above mentioned, there were in the temple some thousands of small images, in gold and silver, of various shapes and dimensions.

The idol destroyed by Mahmood was, in fact, one of the twelve great Lingas, then set up in various parts of India, several of which besides Somesware, or Somanath, which was the name of the Siva demolished by Mahmood, were destroyed by the early Mahommedan conquerors.

In the Kedara Kalpa, Siva says: "I am omnipresent, but I am especially in twelve forms and places.

(1) Somanatha, in Saurashtra. (2) Mallikarjuna, or Sri Saila. (3) Mahakala, in Ougein, (4) Omkara, said to have been in Ujayin. (5) Amareswara, also placed in Ujayin. (6) Vaidyanath, at Deogerh in Bengal. (7) Ramesa, at Setubandha. (8) Bhimasankara, in Dakini. (The 9th is missing from the list enumerated by Mr. Wilson in the Asiatic Researches, said to be unknown). (10) Tryambaka, on the banks of the Gomati. (11) Gautamesa, site unknown. (12) Kedaresa, or Kedaranath, in the Himalaya.

One of the forms in which the Linga worship appears, is that of the Lingayets, Lingawauts, or Jangamas. These are the anti-braminical worshippers of Siva, who are distinguished by their wearing a small idol, either hung on the breast, round the neck or arm, or placed in the turban; the idol is of silver or copper. In common with the Saivas, generally the Jangamas smear their foreheads with Vibhuti or ashes, and wear necklaces and rosaries of the Rudraksha seed. The priests stain their garments with red ochre. They have never been very numerous in the north of India, being rarely met with except as beggars, leading about a bull, the living type of Nandi, the bull of Siva, decorated with housings of various colours and strings of Cowri shells: the conductor carries a bell in his hand, and thus accompanied goes about from place to place, subsisting upon alms. These are the disciples of Basava, whom they regard as a form of the god Siva. They are numerous in the South of India, among the Canarese, the Telugus, and the Tamils, the officiating priests of the Saiva shrines are generally of this sect, when they bear the designations of Aradyha, and Pandaram. The sect is also known by the name of Vira Saiva.

Many years ago, Professor Wilson supplied certain information relative to this sect in his paper in the 17th volume of the Asiatic

Researches. That information was sufficiently interesting to create a desire for further particulars. Additional researches were accordingly entered upon and we are now able to supply a much fuller account than had hitherto been possible.

Among Brahmins the Smartas (followers of Sancar Achari) are generally called saivites, but are in fact freethinkers, equally willing to adore Siva and Vishnu. Their creed may be found in the Mahabharat, the Bhagavat, and the Ramayan, all of which are entirely rejected by the disciples of Basava. There are indeed some few Siva Brahmins who officiate as priests in the Siva temples, and though but little is known of their peculiarities they certainly are different from the Smartas, who refuse to receive the holy water and rice.

The Vira-Saivas are divided into two sects : one is semi-braminical, called Aradhyas ; the other is anti-braminical, and is called Jangam. The Aradhyas claim to be descendants of saivite brahmins, and between them and the Smartas there is a certain degree of reluctant intercourse : founded upon the rites of initiation which both parties use. Their history, when divested of fabulous decoration seems to be that, their creed was founded by Basava, whom they adore as their one deity ; looking upon him as an avatar or incarnation of Siva, the god of this creed.

Basava was the son of a Saivite brahmin, named Madenga Madamantri, at Hinguleswaram, a village near Bagwari in Belgaum, in the southern Mahratta country. When he was a boy he refused (they allege) to wear the braminical thread, because the rites that confer this mark of initiation require the adoration of the sun in the manner prescribed in the Vedas. Perhaps in truth he did assume it, but if so, he subsequently renounced it. Shortly after this time he escaped from his parents, and accompanied by his sister Acca Nagamma, he fled to Calianum, the capital of the Carnataca country, where the reigning prince was Bizzala or Vijala, a Jaina by religion, whose minister, a brahmin, was Basava's maternal uncle : he bestowed employment on Basava, and ultimately gave him his daughter in marriage. ("This proves," says a writer in the Madras Journal, "in my opinion, though opposed to that of his followers, that he did not lay aside the braminical thread in childhood, for had he done so no brahmin could have given him his daughter in marriage.") At his death Basava succeeded to his office, and gradually usurped great power.

It would seem that at this time he began to compare the opposed statements of Jainas and Bramins, and perceived that both creeds were idolatrous. In the end he determined on getting rid of the braminical priestcraft, and accordingly refused to worship any deity but Siva, whose image, the lingam, is the most ancient idol known among the Hindus.

A writer on the subject says:—"This symbol is as separate from indecency in the Hindu mind as circumcision is to the Mahomedan mind. The Brahmins with their usual love of filth have connected a variety of obscenities with the linga worship, but these are wholly unknown to the Jangams, who look upon this idol just as the catholics do upon a reliquary, with deep veneration

"Hanging a golden stamp about their necks
Put on with holy prayers."

The image erected in the Saiva temples being denominated Sthavara Linga, or the stable image, he denominated this reliquary the Jangama Lingam or Locomotive image: a phrase borrowed from the Vedas, where it is used for living being. Hence he and his followers are denominated Jangams, or living images of the deity.

Basava's determined opposition to the Saivite Brahmins and to the Jainas raised him many enemies; while his bounty to the poor gained him friends equally numerous. At last the prince's jealousy was roused, and a civil war ensued, wherein Bizzala was slain, and this event was soon succeeded by the death of Basava, who, according to his followers was "absorbed into the image," or vanished; while the Jaina account declares that he fled to Capila Sangam, where the Malparba and Krishna rivers meet, about one hundred and four miles west of Bellary.

The name Basava is a very common one among Hindus: the Jangams have taken occasion from their teacher having borne it to feign that he was an incarnation of Nandi or Bassava (the Apis or bull appertaining to Siva or Osiris), and this has been the source of numerous idle legends in the subject.

The Basava Purana after recording the events just alluded to, enumerates various marvellous actions, performed by Basava and several of his disciples, such as converting grains of corn to pearls, discovering hidden treasures, feeding multitudes, healing the sick, and restoring the dead to life, and then gives various anecdotes from which we make a selection.

Basava having made himself remarkable for the profuse bounties he bestowed upon the Jangamas, helping himself from the royal treasury for that purpose, the other ministers reported his conduct to Bijala, who called upon him to account for the money in his charge. Basava smiled, and giving the keys of the treasury to the king, requested him to examine it, which being done, the amount was found wholly undiminished. Bijala thereupon caused it to be proclaimed, that whoever calumniated Basava, should have his tongue cut out.

A Jangama, who cohabited with a dancing-girl, sent a slave for his allowance of rice to the house of Basava, where the messenger saw the wife of the latter, and on his return reported to the dancing-girl the magnificence of her attire. The mistress of the Jangama was filled with a longing for a similar dress, and the Jangama having no other means of gratifying her, repaired to Basava, to beg of him his wife's garment. Basava immediately stripped Gangamba, his wife, and other dresses springing from her body, he gave them all to the Jangama.

A person of the name of Kanapa, who regularly worshipped the image of Ckamreswara, imagining the eyes of the deity were affected, plucked out his own, and placed them in the sockets of the figure. Siva pleased with his devotion, restored his worshipper his eyes.

A devout Saiva named Mahadevala Machaya, who engaged to wash for all the Jangamas, having killed a child, the Raja ordered Basava to have him secured and punished; but Basava declined undertaking the duty, as it would be unavailing to offer any harm to the worshippers of Siva. Bijala persisting, sent his servants to seize and tie him to the legs of an elephant, but Machaya caught the elephant by the trunk, and dashed him and his attendant to pieces. He then proceeded to attack the Raja, who being alarmed, applied to Basava, and by his advice, humbled himself before the offended Jangama. Basava also deprecated his wrath, and Machaya being appeased, forgave the king, and restored the elephant and the guards to life.

A poor Jangam having solicited alms of Kinnaraya, one of Basava's chief disciples, the latter touched the stones about them with his staff, and converting them into gold, told the Jangam to help himself.

The work is also in many places addressed to the Jainas, in the shape of a dialogue between some of the Jangama saints and the members of that faith, in which the former narrate to the latter instances of the superiority of the Saiva religion, and the falsehood of the Jain faith, which appears to have been that of Bijala Raza, and the great part of the population of Kalyana. In order to convert them Ckanta Ramaya, one of Basava's disciples, cut off his head in their presence, and then marched five days in solemn procession through and round the city, and on the fifth day replaced his head upon his shoulders. The Jain Pagodas were thereupon, it is said, destroyed by the Jangamas. It does not appear, however, that the king was made a convert, or that he approved of the principles and conduct of his minister. He seems, on the contrary, to have incurred his death by attempting to repress the extension of the Vira Saiva belief. Different authorities, although they disagree as to the manner in which Bijala was destroyed, concur in stating the fact.

In the city of Kalyana were two devout worshippers of Siva, named Allaya and Madhuvaya. They fixed their faith firmly on the divinity they adored, and assiduously reverenced their spiritual preceptor, attending upon Basava whithersoever he went. The king, Bijala, well knew their merits, but closed his eyes to their superiority, and listening to the calumnious accusations of their enemies, commanded the eyes of Allaya and Madhuvaya to be plucked out. The disciples of Basava, as well as himself, were highly indignant at the cruel treatment of these holy men, and leaving to Jagaddeva, the task of putting Bijala to death, and denouncing imprecations upon the city, they departed from Kalyana—Basava fixed his residence at Sangameswara.

Machaya, Bommidevaya, Kinnara, Kannatha, Kakaya, Masayana, Kolakila, Bommadeva, Kesirajaya, Mathirajaya, and others, announced to the people, that the fortunes of Bijala had passed away, as indicated by portentous signs; and accordingly the crows crowed in the night, jackals howled by day; the sun was eclipsed, storms of wind and rain came on, the earth shook, and darkness overspread the heavens. The inhabitants of Kalyana were filled with terror.

When Jagaddeva repaired home, his mother met him, and told him when any injury had been done to a disciple of the Saiva faith, his fellow should avenge him or die. When Daksha treated Siva with contumely, Parvati threw herself into the flames, and so, under the wrong offered to the saints, he should not sit down contented: thus saying, she gave him food at the door of his mansion. Thither also came Mallaya and Bommaya, two others of the saints, and they partook of Jagaddeva's meal. Then smearing their bodies with holy ashes, they took up the spear, and sword, and shield, and marched together against Bijala. On their way a bull appeared, whom they knew to be a form of Basava come to their aid, and the bull went first, even to the court of the king, goring any one that came in their way, and opening a clear path for them. Thus they reached the court, and put Bijala to death in the midst of all his courtiers, and then they danced, and proclaimed the cause why they had put the king to death. Jugaddeva on his way back recalling the words of his mother, stabbed himself. Then arose dissension in the city, and the people fought amongst themselves, and horses with horses, and elephants with elephants, until, agreeably to the curse denounced upon it by Basava and his disciples, Kalyana was utterly destroyed.

Basava continued to reside at Sangameswara, conversing with his disciples, and communing with the divine Essence, and he expostulated with Siva, saying, ' By thy command have I, and thy attendant train, come upon earth, and thou hast promised to recall us to thy presence when our task was accomplished.' Then Siva and Parvati came forth from the Sangameswara Lingam, and were visible to Basava, who fell on the ground before them. They raised him, and led him to the sanctuary, and all three disappeared in the presence of the disciples, and they praised their master, and flowers fell from the sky, and then the disciples spread themselves abroad, and made known the absorption of Basava into the emblem of Siva.*

A writer in the Madras Literary Journal, upwards of fifty years ago, said that by perusing the books and observing the customs of the Jangams, we might plainly see the grounds of that hatred in which Brahmins held the Jangams. Their leader was the resolute opponent of every braminical principle. The Brahmins inculcated the adoration of many gods. He declared that there was only one sole deity. They venerated goddesses and subordinate beings; they reverenced cows, hawks, monkeys, rats and snakes; they used fasts and feasts, penance and pilgrimage, rosaries and holy water. All these he renounced; he set aside the Vedas which they venerated. They declared Brahmins to be literally gods upon earth, women to be vastly inferior to men in all things, and parias to be utterly abominable. Basava abolished these distinctions. He taught that all men are holy in proportion as they are temples of the great spirit; that by birth all are equal; and amongst those whom the Jangam books describe as saints, we find not a single Brahmin, but many parias and many women. In the braminical writings, women are usually treated in a manner abhorrent to European feelings, but in the Jangama books we find a very different temper.

* See the Mackenzie Collection, vol. 2, Halakanara MSS.

The three words Guru, Linga, Jangam, are said to comprise the creed of the sect, and were evidently intended to disavow every part of the braminical priestly tyranny. This mystic phrase is thus expounded. The image (lingam) is the deity : the Jangam is the wearer or fellow worshipper : and he who breathes the sacred spell in the ear is the Guru. Thus he supplies the link between the god and the worshipper, and ever after is looked upon with affection as the true parent : even more respected than the father according to the flesh. For, says the Jangam, I am one with the deity, and he alone is my father who conferred this unity on me.

"Brahmins frequently allege that the Jangams are a depraved sect, who are guided by the Tantras or heretical books," says Mr. Brown, "but we should not incautiously believe this. The Jangams are in all respects opposed to licentiousness, which is the main-spring of the Tantras. The Jangams came from the west, the Tantricas from the north. The Jangams adore the Linga, and abhor Maia the goddess of delusion (Venus or Cali, as Devi), who is expressly the goddess (Yoni, or Bhaga Malini) of the Tantricas. The Tantricas take no notice of the Lingam ; they adore Betala (the devil), and other malevolent powers. The Jangams honour Siva as Daxina Murti, or the beneficent and loving deity. The Tantricas say they aim at a perfect release from fleshly lusts. The Jangams do the same. But the former being hypocrites pretend to yield to their passions as the path to freedom. Whereas the Vira Saivas call on their votaries to deny themselves in all respects. They attend especially to the rules concerning funerals, marriage, and placing infants in the creed. On all these points the Tantras are silent. The Tantras inculcate the use of flesh, wine, magic and debauchery, the Jangam creed abhors these. The Jangams are an avowed sect ; the Tantricas assume the guise of Smartas. The Jangams train up their children in their creed ; the Tantricas merely admit proselytes. The Jangams are sober, devout and humble ; the Tantricas are debauched, atheistical and proud. The Jangams are rigid puritans : the Tantricas are licentious atheists. Herein their depravity resembles that of the worshippers of Isis in Rome, the St. Simonians in France, the Illuminati, and other philosophers of Germany, the followers of Cagliostro in Italy, and the Nessercahs at Kerrund in Persia."

With a few touches of his felicitous pencil, Shakespeare has given a view of their system, or *philosophy* which is the Sacti Puja or Worship of Power.

> "Thus everything includes itself in Power:
> *Power* into will: will into Appetite:
> And Appetite, an universal wolf,
> So doubly seconded with Will and Power
> Must make perforce an universal prey,
> And, last, eat up himself."   TROILUS I.

Again (ANTONY AND CLEOPATRA, II., 1.)—

> "Let witchcraft join with beauty, lust with both:
> Tie up the libertine in a field of sweets
> Keep his brain fuming," &c.

Indeed, the sottish aspirations of Gonzalo (Tempest, Act II, Scene 1), give a summary of the bacchanalian rites taught in the Tantras. And if the reader has any curiosity regarding their system of magic, he will find it in Dr. Herklot's English translation of the Canom-e-Islam, or customs of the Moosulmans of India.

Knowing the deserved odium that attaches to the Tantras, Brahmins assert that these constitute the Jangam system. But were this the case how does it happen that the Tantra volumes are found only in the possession of Brahmins? The fact is that both parties read the Tantras from motives of curiosity, just as a Protestant might read the Koran without in any point adopting the Mahommedan faith. The Jangams honestly avow, and vindicate all they do, they have no motive for concealment. The Brahmin acts on an opposite principle and assures us that the Jangams are a depraved and senseless set of heretics, who obey the levelling principles of the Tantras, and pay honour to the vilest castes.

It is to be observed that no instance is known of a Vira Saiva acting on the principles laid down in the Tantras. To excuse their aptness to read these abominations they allege that the Tantras belong to their creed because they describe Siva as the great deity, and countenance, as Basava does, the abolition of caste. These are but slender apologies, for such an imitation of the evil example set them by the Brahmins.

The Minda Jangamas or Bachelors are spoken of in various passages of the Lingadhari poems. They are confessed to be libertines, but are devout. They have interviews with (Vesias) courtezans who are likewise devout!!

The following is the received opinion. The Jangams are entirely forbidden to have intercourse with prostitutes: but among the earliest proselytes were some unmarried men, who were permitted by Basava to have intercourse with courtezans who belonged to the sect. These men were called Minda Jangams or libertines, and in the present age there are none; for all are bound either to marriage or to virtuous celibacy.

In the western districts there are prostitutes who are called Basvinis, and are said to be thus devoted by their parents, on their lives being in danger through illness in infancy. Some of these are daughters of Jangams: but all are not so, being children of Hindus of other castes. I have heard of some Jangams in similar cases attempting to remove a child's illness by giving it a braminical name, with a view to appease some god or goddess, whose displeasure is imagined to have caused disease. These statements certainly shew the purity of the creed not to be so complete as its devotees assert.

The Vira Saivas illustrate their creed by a comparison quite in the Hindu style. They say, the guru is the cow: whose mouth is the Jangam or brother in the faith; and the lingam or image is the udder. The cow benefits its owner by means of the udder: but what fills the udder? the mouth. And what connects the mouth and the udder? the body. Accordingly if a Vira Saiva wishes the image to benefit him (that is, if he desires to obtain the favour of the deity), he must feed the mouth—that is sustain and comfort his brethren. And then the blessing will be conveyed to him by means of the teacher. Accordingly the Jangams blame the Aradhyas for neglecting this command, and ask how they can expect the image to nourish them if they neglect to sustain brethren and fellows in the faith, for the Aradhya refuses to look upon any but Aradhyas as brethren.

The strangest part of their legends regarding Siva is that wherein he is represented in the most contemptible light as completely the servant of various worthies or saints. Such stories abound in the Basava Puran but are excluded from the Lila. In these, some personages are represented under most degraded circumstances, as obeying or waiting upon the saint whom the legend extols. Thus in the fourth book of the Basava Puran is a story of a certain "worthy" named Nambi, who by force of faith got Siva so completely into his hands that he employed the god as a mere slave. In another story one of the "worthies" scolded Siva, who was so much alarmed that he slunk round the other side of the image, and ran away into the jungle. Other stories represent this paltry demi-god acting either as a thief or as a receiver of stolen goods, to protect his adorers; and they frequently represent him as acting the part of a pander, at the bidding of one of the worthies.

In apology for these stories Jangams allege that they all establish the necessity of faith as the great means of attaining happiness and miraculous power. "As the Brahmins," say they, "call themselves gods upon earth, we will shew that our worthies are quite a match for them." Accordingly there are many legends to prove that food or the leavings of food blessed by a worthy, can perform all sorts of miracles. For instance, a Brahmin, who, by a curse, had become a swine, ate what a Jangam had spit out and hereby resumed the human form. Elsewhere a Jangam's shoe works miracles.

Ravŭnŭ was once carrying an ŭnadec-lingu from Himalŭyŭ to Lŭnka, in order that he might accomplish all his ambitious schemes against the gods, for it was the property of this stone, also called Kamŭ-lingŭ, to grant the worshipper all his desires, whatever they might be. Shinŭ, however, in permitting him to remove this, his image to Lŭnka, made Ravŭnŭ promise that wherever he let it touch the ground, there it should be set up.

When the gods saw that Ravŭnŭ was carrying this stone to Lŭnka, all their heavens were in an uproar, for they knew that if Ravŭnŭ could do what he pleased, neither Indrŭ nor any other god would be able to sit on his throne. Council after council was held, and appeals to this and to that god made, in vain. At last it was resolved that Vŭrvonŭ should be sent, to cause the sea to enter the belly of Ravŭnŭ, who would thereby be compelled to set the stone down while he discharged his water. (Ravŭnŭ could not continue to hold the lingŭ while in this act, as a person becomes unclean at this time until he has bathed). Vŭrvonŭ accordingly set off, and entered the belly of Ravŭnŭ, as he was carrying the lingŭ on his head, and the latter soon began to feel the effect of his visit. His belly swelled prodigiously, but he went on till he could hold his water no longer. At this moment Indrŭ, in the form of an old Bramhŭn, met him. Ravŭnŭ asked him who he was, and where he was going? The latter told him he was an old Bramhun going home. Ravŭnŭ entreated him to take hold of the lingŭ for a short time, and he would bestow upon him the greatest favours. At length the Bramhŭn consented, and Ravŭnŭ, setting the lingŭ on his head, squat on his hams to ease himself. The Bramhŭn agreed to hold the stone an hour but no longer.

Ravŭnŭ told him he should not keep him half that time. After Ravŭnŭ had thus sat for four hours, the Bramhŭn complained he could hold the stone no longer, and he threw it down,—when the bottom part sunk into patŭlŭ, and the top part remains to this day in a place in the zillah of Beerbhoom, called Voidyŭnathu, which is also the name of this lingŭ, and the river at that place called Khŭrsoo is said to have arisen from the water of Ravŭnŭ. Ravŭnŭ when he arose, seeing what had taken place, full of rage and disappointment, went home : some accounts say, having discovered that the gods had played him this trick, he went and fought with them in the most furious manner.

CHAPTER IV.

Lingam worship in the Sheeve Pouran.

IN the Sheeve Pouran are the following references to lingam-worship. Chapter 38—Particularisation of the Lings the of Seda Sheev; and first of the twelve Jyotee Lings, with the history of the first, called Somentathe. Chapter 40—Of sundry Lings; and of Atree, the Reshee, and his wife Anesoomya, procuring the access of the Ganges in a most extraordinary drought. Chapter 41—Sheev's appearance in Mertye Lok to the Reeshees' wives, with a Ling in his hand, while the husbands were absent. Their curses on returning, in consequence of which Sheev's Ling fell off; and moving along on the ground, burnt wherever it touched. The Deivetas, in despair, applied to Brahma, who advised them to sacrifice to Parvetee, and importune her to assume the correspondent form. She did so, and the two Lings becoming united, have ever since been worshipped under that shape by Brahma, Vishnu, etc. Chapter 67—Krishna worships a Ling for seven months, covering it every day with leaves and flowers, all of which were afterwards thrown into a heap: at the end of that time Sheev appears in the midst of a heap, and his august name was Beleishwer. Chapter 72—More particular account of the Mahatmye of the Sheeve Ratree. The history of a hunter who was converted to religion by the accidental falling of the leaves of a tree, where he had placed himself to shoot deer on a Ling, which had been turned up by the deer's foot: the deer and his whole family had engaged themselves by strong oaths to return and offer themselves as food for the hunter's children, and all kept their promise.

Another.—The attendants of Sheev and Dherma Raj dispute about the property in the soul of a thief, who was slain in stealing the victuals belonging to a sacrifice; but having lighted a lamp on the Vrete Sheeve Ratree, for the mere purpose of distinguishing his prey, the holy act of lighting the lamp was held sufficient to secure his salvation.

Fourth Adhyaye.
Brehma is ordered to create the World.

On the Smerene of these five Mentres which were taught to Vishnu, Shree Meha Deiv, who is the compilation of all perfections, came himself and taught Vishnu other Mentres, and Vishnu taught those Mentres, and the mode of Gyan for them, to Brchma. Brehma, with deep foresight and capacious understanding, having practised the Smerene of all these Mentres in purity of heart, thus addressed his prayers to the majesty of Shree Mcha Deiv.

A distich.

'O thou who knowest both what is present and what is concealed, O thou, who art the understanding of the sinner and the saint, O teach thy devotees the several works which it will please thee to perform, and by what means we may imprint on our obsequious hearts the reflection of thy majestic essence.' Shree Bhegewan, out of the loving-kindness which he exerts towards his devotees, turning himself that way, said, 'Attentively listen: having imprinted the Dhyan of this Ling firmly in your heart, be diligent in the Pooja thereof. From piety and devotion to this Ling shall innumerable benefits redound upon you.' Then addressing himself to Vishnu, he proceeded: 'Perform worship to me with perfect fidelity.' Vishnu, submissively signifying assent with his eyes, and performing Nemeskar, returned for answer:—

'Thou art our Lord and we thy slaves, we live one by one in thy power.'

After this, Shree Mcha Deiv said: 'Having thoroughly impressed your minds with the image of my form, compose all your doubts and perplexities; and since your origin is from Prekreetee, ye are strong and mighty: and I have divided my person into three parts: I have fixed Brehma on my right hand, Vishnu on my left, and myself in the place of the breast. And, whereas your faithful attachment is beyond all bounds; whatever desire ye shall have in your minds, it shall be fulfilled.'—'After that,' said Brehma, 'I and Vishnu, performing Nemeskar, humbly observed, that, having bound ourselves with complete attachment to his munificent service, we were hopeful that we should, under no circumstance or place, ever let slip from our hearts the recollection of his Majesty.'

Distich.

In terms of gracious import he answered: 'Since your creation is for the purpose of producing the world, your request hath obtained its accomplishment; and your Bekt, i.e., adoration, shall ever be firm and orthodox towards me. You must make a Preteema, *i.e.*, my image, of clay, and perform Pooja to it: in which ye shall both consult your own advantage and my contentment. Moreover, another figure in this same form of mine, shall appear from a wrinkle of Bremha's forehead, and be named Roodre, and shall apply to compose the perplexities of the creatures; and he shall possess power not inferior to my own. Between him and me there is no distinction. Thou, too, and Bremha, and Roodre, we are in fact all one form, and in no manner whatsoever is there any difference between us four to be be admitted: except only that there is this one distinction between us, that your origin is from Prekreete and mine is not. Wherefore, keeping this in your minds, be diligent in Dyan to me. The four castes also, which are the Brehmen, the Khshtree, the Vishye, and the Soodre; and the four Ashreme, *i.e.*, the Brehmecharee, the Grehest, trye, the Waneprest, and the Sanyassee; together with all other creatures, shall thou introduce into the field of existence, that they may become capable of Gyan and Aghyan. And to Vishnu he said: 'Be thou the granter and bestower of Mooktee in this world, and that, which in my sight is good, shall appear the same in thine; and whosoever shall admit any doubts herein is no Gyance (*i.e.*, learned in the truths of divinity). And, of the Lings which have been already mentioned, having made one of pearl, another of the dung of a milch cow, a third of gold, and a fourth of clay, and joined them together, be diligent in worshipping them.' After giving these orders he vanished; and the Ling of the Pooja of Shree Meha Deiv made its appearance from that same day. He, who in presence of Ling shall open his mouth in praise of Shree Meha Deiv, is for six months in the form of Shree Meha Deiv. There is no doubt of it.

Fifth Adhyaye.

The Reeshes again mentioned to Soote that, by the particulars of the production of the Ling, their greatest crimes were entirely done away, and they became liberated and redeemed. But the Mahatemye, *i.e.*, the mightiness of Sheev and the production of all creatures, was what they wished more expressly to hear specified. Soot Pouraneeke said: "A mercy on your understanding, for ye have well demanded. The Ling of Seda Sheev, which is Anente and Neergoone, announced to Vishnu, 'All creatures shall employ themselves in worshipping thee, and whosoever shall be in straights and difficulties shall obtain release thence by thy favour. Thou must therefore assume a variety of appearances in the world, and obtain fame and glory by the 'Avetars, and conduct the inhabitants of the world to the degree of liberation. I, also, becoming Roodre, in this very form of mine, will closely attend to the different necessities of those who shall be created and sooth their griefs and calamities. As there is no difference between thee and me, and Dhyan, *i.e.*, thought of me, dwells constantly in thy heart, I, too, will never be forgetful of thy Dhyan : and, whosoever shall be a faithful devotee of mine, and hath at the same time evil thoughts towards thee, I will set aside, all his merits and deserts towards me, and precipitate him to the lowest abyss !' Vishnu also answered, ' O ! Meha Raja, whosoever shall be devoted to my Bhekt, and who, shall in the least instance be deficient of respect to thee, I will hold him guilty of the blackest offence, and dispatch him to hell, nor will release him thence until the universal dissolution of all things.' After that, Vishnu said to Brehma, ' Whenever any difficulty shall shew itself to me, be thou my protector ; and since thou art the most exalted and chief of all the Deivetas, pay attention to all matters both in gross and detail. He who shall acknowledge thee, acknowledgeth me also ; and he, who between us two shall start the least distinction, takes the securest method to fix himself in hell. For the space of one hundred grand years, no obscurity, nor diminuition shall be obtruded on the light of thy being ; and one of thy days, which is composed of four thousand Yoogs, and is called Kelpe ;—for that time, be thou rigorous and absolute.'

Thirty-eighth Adhyaye.
Of the particular Lings of Seda Sheev.

The Reesheeshwers demanded of Soote an account of the Lings of Seda Sheev, that are known upon this part of the earth, and are worthy to be worshipped, and where they are stationed.

Soote answered : The Lings of Seda Sheev are innumerable. The whole earth is replete with them ; and whatsoever is visible is a form or species of Ling. Besides which, no place whatsoever is void of them ; both Paradise and Patal are stocked with them ; and all the Deivetas and Reeshes are occupied in their worship. And those who with complete devotion and entire faith have worshipped them, Bhegewan, for the gratification of such devotees, hath appeared and established himself there, at the desire of his votaries, with a Ling for each particular case of demand.

The Lings which are thus extant over the land, are not to be counted : but of such as are now more especially in repute I shall immediately state to you the twelve Jyotee Lings.

Chapter 44.	1.—On the confines of the country of Soorashtree, on the south side is Somenathe,—a Ling of Soda Shoev.
Chap. 37, 44.	2.—On the mountain Shree-Shile—Mellekarjoone.
Chapter 45.	3.—And in the city of Oojeyeenee—two ; the first Mahakate.
	4.—And the second Omkaree.
Chapter 46.	5.—On the back of the mountain Heemachel is Keidarenathe.
Chapter 47.	6.—And in the Dakshenee is Bheeme Shenker.
Chadter 48.	7.—In Benares is Veesheishmer.
Chapter 52.	8.—And on the bank of the river Gotemee, Treombeke.
Chapter 53.	9.—In Jete Bhoom, Veidenathe.
Chapter 54.	10.—And in the desert belonging to Dareka, Nageishwer.
Chapter 55.	11.—In Leitoo Cendhe, Rameishwer.
Chapter 26.	12.—And on the confines of the Dekshen, adjoining the mountain Geere Deive, Doohshemeishe.

He, who rising early in the morning shall repeat the names of these twelve Jyotee Lings, will be freed from all his crimes, and shall obtain his desires : and whoever, on any particular account, addresses a particular Ling, he will succeed accordingly, and such person is not freed from the crimes by the Dershene, or view of the twelve Jyotee Lings. It is enjoined all the four casts to perform Pooja to those ; and, after Pooja, if they eat the sacrificial morsels they are purified from their crimes on the spot. And if they worship any one of these twelve Jyotee Lings for six months, Mooktee becomes their destiny, and they are no more subject to birth : and, if ever a Meieke, or Chandale, or deceiver, obtains Deersheene of the Jyotee, in another generation he is born in the house of a Veidread Brahmin, and becomes Mookte.

CHAPTER V.

The four kinds of Stone lingas—Siva under a form called Muhakalu—Temporary images of Siva—Siva's wives—Siva's and Parvati's quarrels—Siva and Doorga—Siva's names—The heaven of Siva—Latsami—Power of the priests—Tamil poetry—Indecent worship—Dancing girls at religious ceremonies—Christian and Pagan idolatry—Religious prostitution—Worship of the female—Development of indecent practices—Saktipuja.

MR. WARD informs us that besides the clay images of the linga, there are four kinds of stone lingas which are set up in the Hindu temples. "The first," he says, "is called swuyumbhoo, that is, the self-existent linga. The second is named unadee, or that which has no beginning. (At the time of a great drought, the Hindoos, after performing its worship, throw very large quantities of water upon this unadee-linga, in order to induce Siva to give them rain). The third they call vanu-linga, because a king named Vanu first instituted this worship. The fourth is the common, or factitious linga. These images are all of stone, brought from the neighbourhood of the river Gundhukee, which falls into the Ganges near Patna.

The Hindoos of every caste and of both sexes, make images of the linga with the clay of the river Ganges, every morning, after bathing, and worship it, making bows, presenting offerings, and repeating incantations before it. This is most frequently done by the side of the river.

Besides the linga, there is another form in which Siva is worshipped, called Muhakalu. This is the image of a smoke-coloured boy, with three eyes, his hair standing erect, clothed in red garments, his teeth very large; he wears a necklace of human skulls, and a large juta; in one hand he has a stick, and in another the foot of a bedstead; a half moon appears on his forehead; he has a large belly; and presents a very terrific appearance. Siva is called Muhakalu, because he destroys all, or all is absorbed in him at the time of a kalpu, and afterwards reproduced.

Images of this form of Siva were not made in Bengal, but a pan of water, or an unadee-linga, was substituted, before which bloody sacrifices were offered, and other ceremonies performed, in the month Kartiku, at the new moon.

In the month Phalgoonu, every year, the Hindoos made the image of Siva, and worshipped him for one day, throwing the image the next day into the water. This worship was performed in the night, and was accompanied with singing, dancing, music, feasting, &c. The image worshipped was either that of Siva with five faces or that with one face.

In the month Maghu a festival in honour of Siva is held for one day, when the image of this god, sitting on a bull, with Parvutee his bride on his knee, is worshipped in the principal towns in Bengal.

Siva had two wives, Sutee and Parvutee. Sutee was the daughter of king Dukshu, and Parvutee the daughter of the mountain Himaluyu.

The fourth chapter of the Shreebhaguvutu, contains the history of Dukshu, the son of Brahma; of his daughter Sutee, who was married to the god Siva; of the abuse of Siva by Dukshu; of Siva's cursing Dukshu; of the grand sacrifice of Dukshu; the gods all arrive at this sacrifice; the daughters of Dukshu are also present; Sutee wishes to go, but is forbidden of Siva her husband; Siva, however, at last consents to her going; she goes, and while her father is abusing her husband, she dies of grief; Siva on hearing of the death of his wife, was transported with rage, and taking his juta from his head, threw it on the ground with great force, and up sprang a monster, in the form of a sunyasee, covered with ashes, having three flaming eyes, with a trishoolu in his hand, wearing a tiger's skin, and a necklace of human bones; and having a round red mark like a ball betwixt his eyebrows; this monster asked Siva why he created him; Siva ordered him to go and destroy Dukshu; this monster then took along with him armies of pratus, bhootus, yukshus, pishacus, etc. (wandering spirits), and destroyed Dukshu's sacrifice; Siva's great sorrow at the loss of Sutee; the gods come to comfort him; Sutee is again born; her father's name Heemaluyu, her mother's Manuku; Dukshu, after repairing the injuries which Siva's juta-formed monster had made, completes his sacrifice, etc.

A number of stories are contained in some of the Hindoo books respecting the quarrels of Siva and Parvutu, some of them arising out of the revels of the former, and the jealousy of the latter. These quarrels resemble those of Jupiter and Juno. The chief fault of Juno is said to have been jealousy. When Siva and Parvatu quarrelled, she frequently upbraided him with his filthy condition as a yogee. When they were about to be married, the mother of the girl, and the neighbours poured the utmost abuse on Siva: the neighbours cried out, "Ah! ah! ah! this image of gold, this most beautiful damsel, like whom there is hardly such a beauty in the three worlds, to be given in marriage to such a fellow—an old fellow with three eyes; without teeth; clothed in a tiger's skin; covered with ashes; encircled with snakes; with a necklace of human bones; with a human skull in his hand; with a filthy juta, viz., a bunch of hair like a turban, twisted round his head; who chews intoxicating drugs; has inflamed eyes; rides naked on a bull, and wanders about like a madman. Ah! they have thrown this beautiful daughter into the river!" In this manner the neighbours exclaimed against the marriage, till at last, Narudu, who had excited this hubbub, settled the matter, and the wedding was consummated.

On a certain occasion Siva ordered his servants Nundee and Bhringee to prepare his bull that he might go a-begging; he himself bound the rag round his loins, twisted snakes as ornaments round his wrists, made a poita of three other snakes; put a tiger's skin on his back, a drum and a trident in his right hand, and in his left a horn; his body was covered with ashes. Thus arrayed he mounted his bull, Nundee going before and Bhringee behind, and went into different places begging from door to door. Wherever he went, he saw the people happy and contented, enjoying all the pleasures of life. At the sight of all this happiness, Siva was full of grief, and said in his mind, "All these people are surrounded with their friends and children, and are happy; but after marrying, I have obtained nothing. I beg for my daily bread." Having collected a little rice, etc., Siva returned home, full of vexation. Doorga, his wife, gave him water to wash his feet, and Siva ordered her to prepare an intoxicating beverage called siddhee, and asked her whether she had prepared his food? She told him that she had not yet kindled the fire. "What!" said Siva, "it is now two o'clock in the afternoon, and you have not begun to prepare the dinner?" Filled with anger, he began to use the most violent language: "How is this? I have married a wife destitute of fortunate signs, and I spend my life in misery. I see other families have bathed and sit down to dinner by noon. I beg three times a day, and yet I cannot obtain sufficient to support nature. It has always been said in the three worlds, that he who obtains a lucky wife, will through her become rich; through a lucky husband, sons are born. See now (addressing himself to those present), I have two sons; but where are the riches which a fortunate wife procures? I suppose that in marrying the wife of Himaluyu (a mountain) every one is become hard as the rock towards me. In constantly begging I have obtained the name of Shunkuru, the beggar. A person marrying a lucky wife sits at his ease in his house, and eats excellent food, and I go a-begging, and yet starve. Narudu has given me such an unlucky wife, what shall I say to him, a fellow without ancestry? He is not content unless he insult the dead. I can no longer support my family by begging. I can support myself, but how, can I provide for so many?"

Doorga, hearing all this, was full of sorrow, and began to utter her grief to her two maids Juya and Vijuya: "Hear! without thought, why does he abuse me in this manner? If he call me an unlucky wife, why did he marry me? When a person's fate is bad, they say his forehead is on fire. Why does he call me unlucky? Is not his own forehead on fire, and are we not suffering through his bad fate? True, I have neither a beautiful form, nor excellent qualities, nor conduct, nor honour, nor wisdom, nor learning, nor property, nor race, nor brother, nor friend, nor father, nor mother, nor relations, nor ornaments; but, look at his form; he covers himself with the ashes of the dead; at his qualities; he is known as the smoker of intoxicating herbs (the drunkard); at his conduct; he resides in cemeteries, and dwells with the bhootus;—at his wisdom: amidst the assembled guests at his wedding he sat naked; rides on a bull, and is hooted at by the children in the streets as a fool;—at his learning; he does not know the names of his father and mother; at his property, he owns a bull, a drum, and a tiger's skin;—at his ornaments: he is covered with snakes;—at his honour: at the time of marriage he was not able to obtain anything richer than a tiger's skin for a garment, though he begged for something better. It is true he has had two sons born, and on this account, I suppose, he is filled with pride. But such sons, in the three worlds, were never born before, and I hope will never be born again. Behold his eldest son Kartiku, he drinks intoxicating beverage like his father; he is full of rage if his food be delayed but a moment; what his father begs, he, with his six mouths, devours; the peacock that carries him devours the snakes with which his father clothes himself; his other son Gunashu has four arms, an elephant's head, and eats like an elephant; he is carried by a rat, which steals and eats the unshelled rice brought by Siva. Thus the children and the father are equally forsaken of fortune. The companions of Siva are either ghosts or bhootus."

As soon as Siva had mounted his bull to go a-begging, Doorga said to Juya and Vijuya, "I will stay no longer here. He tells me to keep my hair clothed with dirt, and to cover my body with ashes. I will go to my father's house, come along." The maids endeavoured to pacify her, and to shew her the danger of leaving her husband. After a number of expostulations, she was persuaded to assume the form of Unnu-poorna, by which means the wealth of the whole world flowed into her lap. She gave a splendid entertainment on mount Koilasu to all the gods, at the close of which Siva arrived from a begging journey. Struck with astonishment at what he saw, he was wonderfully pleased, and ate for once till he was nearly surfeited. When he and Doorga were sitting together on the evening of this feast, he apologised to his wife for the unkind language he had used towards her, to prevent which in future, he proposed that they should be united in one body. Doorga at first strongly objected, but was at length persuaded to consent, and Siva and Doorga became one, the right side (white) being Siva, and the left side (yellow) Doorga. In this form an image is annually worshipped in Bengal.

Other stories are told of Siva's descending to earth in the form of a sunyasee, for the preservation of some one in distress, or to perform religious austerities.

Amongst the fanciful names (a thousand in number) belonging to this god, are the following :—Siva, the benefactor—Muhashwuru, the great god—Ceshwuru, the glorious god—Chundrushakuru, he on whose forehead is seen a half-moon—Bhootashu, he who is lord of the bhootus—Miriru, he who purifies—Mirityoonjuyu, he who conquers death—Krittivasa, he who wears a skin—Oogru, the furious—Shree-kuntu, he whose throat is beautiful—Kupalubhrit, he whose alms dish is a skull—Smuruhuru, the destroyer of Kama-davu, the god of love—Tripoorantuku, he who destroyed an usooru named Tripooru—Gungadhuru, he who caught the goddess Gunga in his bunch of hair—Vrishudhwuju, or he who rides on a buil—Shoolee, he who wields the Trident—St'hanoo, the everlasting—Survu, he who is everything—Gireeshu, lord of the hills—Undhuku-ripoo, he who destroyed an usooru named Undhuku—Sunkurshunu, he who destroys the world—Trilochunu, the three-eyed—Ruktupu, the drinker of blood—Siddhusavitu, the drinker of an intoxicating beverage called Siddhe.

The work called Krityu-tuttwu describes the heaven of this god as situated on the mountain Koilasu, and called Shivu-pooru. It is said to be ornamented with many kinds of gems and precious things, as pearls, coral, gold, silver. On the mountain reside gods, the heavenly choristers, dancers and courtezans, gods who act as servants to the other gods, sacred sages, divine sages, great sages, and a number of moonees. These persons constantly perform the worship of Siva and Doorga, and the upsurus are continually employed in singing, dancing, etc. The flowers of every season are always in bloom here, the winds shvityu, sangundu, and mandyu —gentle winds accompanied with coolness and sweetness—always blow on these flowers, and diffuse their fragrance all over the mountain wherein many birds are constantly singing and repeating the names of Doorga and Siva, where the waters of the heavenly Ganges pass along in purling streams, where the six seasons—the spring, the summer, the rainy, the sultry, the dewy, the cold—at once exist, and where on a golden throne, adorned with jewels, sit Siva and Doorga, holding conversation, in which Doorga asks questions of her husband.

"When the mountain Mervuva was whirled about in the sea, the motion produced a foam which was like the cradle of a beautiful woman named Latsami. This second Venus was bestowed on Vishnuvu, preferably to the Devetas, who were all in love with her. The Scivias, who assert that Eswara is the sovereign God, say also, that he has a wife called Parvati. They tell us that she had a double birth; first she was daughter to Datsja, son of Brahma, and of Sarasvati his wife. Her father gave her in marriage to Eswara, and some time after intended to perform a Jagam or sacrifice, to which he invited the Devetas, such as Denendre, the Sun, the Moon, and the rest, but neglected Eswara, his son-in-law. Parvati told him he should also have invited him, but he, instead of agreeing with her, made her the following injurious answer:— Eswara, says Datsja is not worthy of that honour, he is a fellow that subsists only on alms, and has no clothes to put on. We are to suppose that Eswara was at that time *incog.*, and veiled under such a shape as made him unknown to all. Parvati inflamed with rage, cried out to her father, I myself am therefore not worthy to assist at it; and saying these words, she leaped into the fire that was prepared for this solemnity. Eswara, exasperated in the highest degree at this unhappy accident, was all over in a sweat, and one of the drops of it happening to fall on the earth, Virrepadra sprung from it, who immediately asked his father what commands he had for him. Eswara bid him go and destroy the Jagam of Datsja, and was obeyed; for he killed some of the guests, drove away others, cut off Datsja's head, kicked the sun, and broke all his teeth, so that he had not one left, and drubbed the moon so heartily, that her face was covered all over with the marks of the blows he gave her, which continue to this day. The Devetas implored Eswara's mercy, and obtained it; he was softened by their entreaties, and restored Datsja to life, on whose body he fixed the head of a he-goat instead of his own. Parvati being consumed in the fire into which she had thrown herself, was indulged a new birth, and was daughter of the mountain Chimawontam, who married her to Eswara. Her husband was so passionately in love with her, that he gave her half his body, so that she became half man and half woman; for which reason the Brahmins call her Andhanari-Eswara, a name implying such an union.

These people are of opinion, that both Vishnu and Eswara can procreate children without the commerce of the other sex, since they ascribe to them a power of getting them by the bare act of the will, so that they suppose they only have them for dalliance sake. Eswara is represented in the temples under a very immodest shape, expressing by an action, the union of both sexes. This is grounded on a tradition which the Brahmins themselves are partly ashamed of, and is as follows: It fell out one day that a Moniswara came to visit Eswara in a place where the latter used to caress Parvati. The Moniswara came at a very unseasonable hour; in vain the porter shut the gate upon him, and even told him the reason why he could not be admitted; for the Maniswara was so enraged to find he must be forced to stay till Eswara should please to show himself, that he broke out into an imprecation, which he immediately repented of. Eswara had overheard him, but pardoned him when he found he was sorry for it. The Moniswara, not satisfied with being pardoned for his offence, requested that all who should worship the image of Lingam—the figure representing the union of the sexes in the manner above mentioned, should reap greater advantages from it than if they were to worship Eswara when represented with his whole body. He obtained his desire, and it is to this circumstance that those scandalous images under which Eswara is worshipped in the Pagods, owe their original.*

Mahadeu signifies the sovereign God. He is represented under

---

* Picard, Ceremonies et Coutumes Religieuses.

the shape of a pillar which diminishes insensibly from its base to its extremity at top. It is evident that this figure is the same as the Priapus of other nations; and that the modern Indians, as well as those of antiquity, have equally considered it as the God of Nature. Pictures which have reached us from India exhibiting the interiors of the Pagods of Mahadeu reveal beyond all doubt the nature of this pillar; it cannot be mistaken for any else than what we have just suggested, viz., the male organ of generation. It is of gigantic size, rising many feet from the floor, and the most profound veneration is rendered to it by the worshippers who completely uncover their feet before passing the threshold.

Ixora (Mahadeu) bears also the name of Lingam. The Jogins wear the Lingam about their necks; but it would be impossible for fancy, says Picard, to invent anything more obscene, than the posture in which they represent this double figure, to whom they assiduously offer the first fruits of their meals. We ascribe to the notion the Indians entertain that everything is formed by generation, the blind devotion they pay to this Lingam, in which they confound the agent with the means he employs. It will be impossible to justify them in any manner on this head, but by considering it as a type or symbol, which still cannot but be shocking to decency and good manners; some, however, cannot help thinking that those who first invented these figures, were naturally inclined to satiate by lust, what they exhibited for the emblem of a Deity.

"It cannot be denied, but that the worship which is paid to nature, may have migrated from the east into the west, together with the symbolical figures under which they represented it; we are therefore not to wonder, that the same idea should have discovered itself under different names, to people who live at a great distance one from the other; since, as they both received the object of their worship from the same source, they were under a necessity of receiving the same images with the same ceremonies. To do these people justice, nothing can better express the fruitfulness of nature than the union of both sexes, and the vigour of Priapus, whose name is very expressive; however, it is surprising that men, who, if we except some of the most brutal savages, have always paid some regard to decency, should be so lost to all sense of it, as to carry in procession with great pomp and solemnity, those parts of the body, which ought never to be revealed but in cases of the highest necessity; and expose them publicly in the roads, in houses and temples, as is the custom in India." *

* Picard, Ceremonies et Coutumes Religieuses.

Pietro Dello Valle, observes, that the gods of the Indians are always represented naked, and that several figures in very indecent postures are seen in the pagods; undoubtedly he saw the Lingam above-mentioned there. The other figures might possibly represent the vows or homages of the devout Indians, among whom the women do not scruple to prostitute themselves in honour of the gods. Husbands behold with the most profound humility these meritorious prostitutions, which so often revive what we in Europe look upon as the greatest injury and affront; so true it is, that false principles in religion easily destroy those of common decency, and even frequently change the very ideas which nature has implanted in us. As a husband is fully persuaded he has been cuckolded by a god, he is therefore very well satisfied. The Jognis s the idol's curate, and performs the ceremony in quality of his proxy, while the devoutly patient husband, in the meantime, washes the saint's feet, and pays him the utmost veneration. The people of the house withdraw, and leave the lady to the saint's embraces. When this institution was made, the crafty Indians undoubtedly insinuated some hopes of future felicity at the same time. When we have once found out the secret of gaining an ascendant over people's minds, can it be a difficult matter to assure the female devotees, that,

> *Si quelque chose les empêche*
> *D'aller tout droit en paradis,*
> *C'est d'epargner pour leurs maris,*
> *Un bien dont ils n'ont plus que faire,*
> *Quand ils ont pris leur necessaire.*
>
> La Fontaine dans ses Contes.

The sense of which is,

If anything prevents their being immediately wafted to Paradise, 'tis to reserve for their husbands a pleasure which they have no farther occasion for, when they have had their quantum of it.

We mention an instance which manifestly shews, that the Indians look upon the obscene devotions just alluded to, as highly meritorious. Over the gate of one of the cities of the little kingdom of Sirinpatan, says Dellon in the preface to his Voyages, printed in 1709, stands a stone statue representing Sita, wife to Ram, one of their gods, about as big as the life. On each side of her are three famous Faquirs, or Penitents, naked, on their knees, their eyes lifted up towards her, and holding with both hands what decency will not permit me to mention. They pretend by this posture, to pay such an homage, at they judge to be most grateful to this pretended goddess.*

Mr. R. C. Caldwell, writing in Johnson's Universal Cyclopædia, says :—" Of old, pious Hindus who spiritualised their religion, even the grossest forms of it, linga-worship included, were not lacking. For instance, the great Tamilian poet, Sivavakkiar, writes as follows (see the Indian Antiquary, Bombay, Apr., 1872, first paper on Tamil Popular Poetry) :

" My thoughts are flowers and ashes,
In my breast's fane enshrined,
My breath, too, is therein it,
A linga unconfined :
My senses, too, like incense
Rise, and like bright lamps shine,
There, too, my soul leaps ever
A dancing god divine."

This, is my opinion, is one of the finest stanzas penned by Sivavakkiar. The drift of it is this :—You popular Hindus, you have your temples,—you have your flowers, and sacred ashes,—you have your phallus, or emblem of divine creative power,—you have also your incense and lamps, and you have your divine dancer, Siva. I, too, have my flowers and ashes, but they are of the mind ! I, too, have my linga, but it is my breath or spirit. I, too, have my incense and lamps, but they are my five senses. And I, too, have my deity leaping in divine sport within me, but that is my soul. In a word, mine is the true spiritual worship.

" Here the sage speaks of his body as a metaphorical temple (using language similar to that employed in the New Testament, ' Ye are the temples of the Holy Ghost'); then he likens his thoughts to flowers and ashes, which are used in the services of temples ; lastly, he declares that his breath or spirit—which as a part of universal life has no bound or limit—is the true *linga*, creative, and a part of the creation, of his own being."

The serious consequences of adopting erroneous principles, even such as are commonly called metaphysical ones, seemingly the most remote from practice, is perhaps in nothing more apparent than with respect to the ideas which were in early ages entertained concerning *nature*, when its attributes came to be objects of

* Picard, Ceremonies et Contumes Religieuses.

worship. As there must be a concurrence of male and female powers for the production of all living creatures, it was supposed that, in the great productive powers of nature, there must be both male and female qualities. The Egyptians had this idea, and accordingly several of their principal deities were said to be both male and female. Having little idea of delicacy, they represented those powers by the figures of the parts of generation. The constant exhibition of these figures in their religious worship could not but lead to much lewdness, first as an act of religion, acceptable to their gods, and then in common life; though this might be far from the intention of those who formed the plan of the popular worship.

Hence, however, it is that, in the ancient heathen religions, we find rites of the most opposite nature, the extreme of severity and cruelty in some, and the extreme of indecency and sensual indulgence in others. This is well known to have been the case in Egypt, the mother of religion and of science, to a great part of the Western world. We cannot without the utmost disgust and horror think of what, according to the testimony of Herodotus, whose authority in this case cannot be questioned, women did before the bull Apis, and especially with the goat that was worshipped at Mendes, to say nothing of the peculiarly indecent manner in which he says that in their religious processions, they carried the phalli, and of their behaviour; when, in some of their festivals, they went in boats along the Nile, and exhibited themselves to the inhabitants of the villages on its borders. The Nile itself, according to the testimony of Christian writers, was worshipped with the most obscene and execrable rites, even Sodomitical practices.

The idea that Plutarch gives us of the Egyptian rites is sufficiently disgusting. "Many of their religious ceremonies," he says, "were of a mournful cast, and celebrated with much austerity. Some of their festivals and direful sacrifices were considered as unfortunate and mournful days, and were celebrated by eating raw flesh, torn with men's nails. On other days they fast, and smite their breasts, and in several places filthy and indecent words are used during the sacrifices. In their festivals and processions, the greater part act ludicrous things both, speaking and thinking words of the most wicked and lewd meaning, and that even of the gods themselves. But when they consult their oracles they are advised to have pious thoughts in their hearts, and words of good sound in their mouths."

No revels of the most irreligious persons could be more extravagant and indecent than the festivals of Bacchus; and the same people who sacrificed men, and even their own children, had places appropriated to prostitution, even of both sexes, adjoining to their temples, the profits arising from which were a part of their revenues.

The Hindoo religion has much in it in this respect, that is similar to that of the ancient Egyptian. "Nothing," says De la Crose, "is more revered by the Hindoos than the lingam. Their most solemn worship is presented to their gods in this form. Lighted lamps are continually burning before it, in the inmost recesses of their temples, surrounded by other lamps with seven branches, like that of the Hebrews. Besides those in the temples, they have small ones of stone or crystal, which they hang to their necks, and fasten upon their heads. To these they address almost all their prayers, and frequently have them buried with them."

Captain Campbell, after describing the lascivious dancing of Hindoo girls, who get their living by it, says, "that such enticements to vice should make a part of the system of any society is to be lamented: yet in all ceremonies and great occasions, whether religious worship or domestic enjoyment, they make a part of the entertainment; and the altars of their gods, and the purity of the magic rites, are alike polluted by the introduction of the dancing girls. The impurity of this custom, however, vanishes, when compared with the hideous practice of introducing dancing boys."

With respect to the pagoda of Jaggernat, which he calls a curious and grotesque monument of superstitious folly, he says, "it is an immense barbarous structure of a kind of pyramidal form, embellished with devices cut in stone work, not more singular than disgusting."

Christian idolaters, in forming types and figures of divine things, always endeavour to represent them with personal beauty, as proportionate to their divine nature as human skill can make it. Those Pagans, on the contrary, in forming their idols, cast out every vestige of beauty—everything that, by the consent of mankind, is supposed to convey pleasing sensations; and, in their place, substitute the most extravagant, unnatural deformity, the most loathsome nastiness, the most disgusting obscenity. It is not in language to convey an adequate idea of their temples and idols; and if it was, no purpose could be answered by it, only the excitement of painful and abominable sensations. To keep pace with the figures of their idols, a chief Brahmin, by some accursed artificial means (by herbs, I believe), has brought to a most unnatural form, and enormous dimensions, that which decency forbids me to mention ; and the pure and spotless women who from infancy have been shut up from the sight of men, even of their own brothers, are brought to kiss this disgusting and misshapen monster, under the preposterous belief that it promotes fecundity.

Tavernier mentions the same abominable custom, as also does Alexander Hamilton, in his account of the East Indies.

In this pagoda, Capt. Campbell says, stands the figure of Jaggernat, but it is nothing more than a black stone of an irregular pyramidal form, having two rich diamonds in the top by way of eyes, and a nose and mouth painted red. For this god, he says, five hundred priests are employed in spoiling food.

Every pagoda, says La Crose, has a certain number of prostitutes annexed to it, dedicated to its use by pompous and solemn ceremonies. They choose the handsomest, and educate them in such a manner, that when they come to a proper age they may bring the greatest gain to the temple by the price of their prostitution. They can never marry, or leave the idol; and their children, if they have any, are also dedicated to it.

Some, says Mr. William Chambers, devote their own children to this profession. This is customary in the Decan, but not with the Hindoos of Bengal or Hindoostan proper. He says this custom was probably derived from the religion of Buddha. But almost all the ancient heathen religions had the same custom. It is described at large by Herodotus, as it was practised at Babylon in his time; and it is frequently alluded to in the Old Testament. Lucian in his Treatise on the Syrian goddess, says that those women who refuse to cut off their hair on her festival, must prostitute themselves during one day ; and that what they receive on that account is given to the goddess for a sacrifice. In Malabar it is reckoned meritorious to bring up girls, who are commonly bastards, for the service of the temples, and they are taught music and dancing. When they are of a proper age, they go through the ceremony of a marriage to the god.

The Shastrus declare that the daughters of Brahmins, till they are eight years old, are objects of worship as forms of the goddess Bhagavatee. Many persons performed the worship of these girls daily. They took the daughter of some neighbouring brahmin, and placing her on a seat, with flowers, paint, water, garlands, etc., performed her worship, and then presented to her, if they were rich, offerings of cloth, ornaments, etc. At the close, the worshipper offered incense, and prostrated himself before this girl. At the worship of some of the female deities also, the daughters of Brahmins have divine honours paid to them. Many of the Tantra Shastrus, and particularly the Roodru'yamulu, the Yoni-tantra, and the Neelu-tantra, contain directions for a most extraordinary and disgusting puja, which is understood in a private manner amongst the Hindoos by the name of Chukru.

These Shastrus direct that the person or persons who wish to perform this puja must first, in the night, take a woman as the object of worship. If the person who performs this worship be a dukshinacharu, he must take his own wife, and if a vamacharu, he must take the daughter of a dancer, a kupalee, a washerman, a barber, a chundalu, or of a mussulman, or a prostitute, and place her on a seat or mat; and then bring boiled fish, flesh, fried peas, rice, spirituous liquors, sweetmeats, flowers, and all the other offerings and things necessary for the puja. These offerings, as well as the female, must next be purified by the repeating of incantations. To this, succeeds the worship of the person's guardian deity; and after this the worship of the female, with all the ceremonies included in the term puja. The female must be naked during the worship .... Here indecencies not fit to be recorded in the present age and country, are contained in the directions of the shastru for this worship, relating to every part of the body in turn. Ward said that the learned Brahmin who opened to him these abominations, made several efforts—paused and began again, and then paused again, before he could pronounce the shocking indecencies prescribed by his own shastrus.

As the object of the worship was a living person, at the close of the puja she partook of the offerings in the presence of the worshipper or worshippers. Hence she drank of the spirituous liquors, ate of the flesh, though it was that of the cow, and also of the other offerings. The orts were to be eaten by the person or persons present, while sitting together, however different their castes may be, nor might any one despise any of the offerings, or refuse to eat of them; the spirituous liquors were to be drunk by measure. The company while eating had to put food also in each other's mouths.

Ward wrote:—"The person who performs the ceremonies, in the presence of all, behaves towards this female in a manner which decency forbids to be mentioned. The persons present must then perform puja in a manner unutterably abominable, and here this most diabolical business closes. At present persons performing these abominations are becoming more and more numerous. They are called vamacharees. In proportion as these things are becoming common, so much the more are the ways of performing them more and more beastly. They are done in secret : but that these practices are becoming very frequent among the Brahmins and others is a fact known to all. The persons who perform these actions agreeably to the rules of the Shastrus are very few. The generality do those parts that belong to gluttony, drunkenness and whoredom only, without being acquainted with all the minute rules and incantations of the shastrus."

Pratapuchandra Ghosha, in reading a paper before the Asiatic Society of Bengal, in September, 1870, said :—" In the earliest portraits of the Aryan race, as delineated in the Vedas, we find their ideas and their thoughts centred in their homes, their cattle, their fields, and in the discomfiture of their enemies. Their wants were few, and their prayers, therefore, were less varied ; and their ceremonies were, probably, equally simple. But this simplicity wore within itself the seed of a very complex system of thought. Everything that was useful in some way or other, everything that was beautiful or awful in nature, or that excited unusual feelings, or suggested new ideas, was estranged from the ordinary and associated with the supernatural. A new current of thought soon after set in. In the freshness of imagination during the primitive state of society, comparisons, metaphors, and allegories, were soon changed into real entities, and mythology rapidly gained ground in men's minds. Thus, the Puranas, by a natural poetical idea, made the sun and the moon, which witness all that is done on the earth, the spies of the divine ruler—a myth describing the all-pervading nature of their rays. In the Vedas, they are regarded as the universal witnesses of all ceremonies. The Rahu, the ascending node, is derived from the verb literally meaning to abandon, void, hence also black, darkness, shadow, etc., and is represented in mythology as having no body, the *umbra* of the astronomers. The *umbra* may be said to devour as it were the luminaries. Later mythology makes Rahu a trunkless head, an ingenious mythological adaptation of the umbra which devours, but inasmuch as it has no body, the moon comes out from the throat. Again, poetic imagination or extreme fear, personifies qualities, and that to such an extraordinary extent, that while describing the bloodthirsty vengeance of Sakti, she is said to have, in the *Chhinnamasta* incarnation, cut off her own head from the trunk, and with the gaping trunkless skull gluttonously drank her own blood which springs with the warmth of life. However hideous the conception is, it is the result of the license allowed to poets to use partial similitudes. To such flights of unshackled imagination, the variously formed sphinxes of the Chaldeans are but mere flutters of the wings. As allegories illustrative of the concentration of force to overcome difficulties, and the adaptation of means to a purpose, the achievements of Durga offer many interesting instances. On the occasion of vanquishing the mighty *Asuras*, Sumbha and Nisumbha, and their general, named Mahishásura (the buffaloe-demon), the several gods are made to direct their energy to their weapons for the purpose. The goddess Durga, representative of this union, sprung forth with ten arms, fit to crush several *Asuras* at one fell swoop. Káli, another incarnation of Sakti, in the war with Raktavija, a demon multiplying his race, as his name implies, from the drops of blood flowing from his body, and touching the earth, is represented as having licked up the blood as it streamed forth from his person with a view to arrest that dreadful propagation.

Many of these myths, again, may be traced partly to oriental hyperbole, and partly to the many-sided meanings of the words used in describing them: figurative expressions were seized and new myths were invented in illustration of them. Others again are illustrative of national customs; thus the protruded tongue of Káli has been the theme of several fanciful tales. With some, in the heat of the battle, Káli was so maddened, that the gods despaired of the world, and sent Siva, her husband to appease her. Siva crept among the dead soldiers lying in the field, and contrived to pass under the feet of Káli, who no sooner perceived her husband trampled under her feet, than she became abashed, and in the fashion of the women of the country, bit her tongue as expressive of her regret and indelicacy.

It is amusing to follow the line of argument put forth in the Puranas in support of these myths. In some instances, they approach so near the ludicrous, that were it not for their thorough adaptability to the state of native society of the time, their fallacies would have been long ago exposed, and the whole Puranic system spurned and despised.

Sakti is Force. Originally a sect of Hindoos worshipped force and matter as eternal. The word being in the feminine gender. its personification is a female divinity of supernatural powers, and every occupation which called for great exercise of energy and power at once selected her as tutelary goddess, and she is now the most popular of all the three and thirty millions of the Hindu pantheon. *Saktaism* has since imbibed so many brutal practices of cannibalism, human sacrifices, and bacchanalian rites, that the very name of a Sakta, inspires horror and disgust, nevertheless the unholy Tantras, which propound and explain the principles of this doctrine, and give rules for worshipping the different forms of Sakti, are increasing in number and popularity. They were, until lately, comparatively unknown beyond the frontier of Bengal, but copies of MSS. are now demanded from every quarter of Hindustan. The Tantric system is of Bengali origin, and its rites and customs are ultimately interwoven with those of the hill tribes, especially those of Nepal and Assam. Demonology is a principal feature in the Sakta faith, and the various nocturnal ceremonies are fixed which were much in vogue in Bengal, even as late as about fifty years ago."

The great feature of the religion taught by the Tantras is the worship of Sakti—Divine power personified as a female, and individualised, not only in the goddesses of mythology, but in every woman : to whom, therefore, in her own person religious worship may be and is occasionally addressed. The chief objects of adoration, however, are the manifold forms of the bride of Siva ; Parvati, Uma, Durga, Kali, Syama, Vindhya-vasini, Jaganmata, and others. Besides the usual practices of offerings, oblations, hymns, invocations, the ritual comprises many mystical ceremonies and accompaniments, gesticulations and diagrams, and the use in the commencement and close of the prayers of various monosyllabic ejaculations of imagined mysterious import. Even in its last exceptionable division it comprehends the performance of magical ceremonies and rites, intended to obtain super-human powers, and a command over the spirits of heaven, earth, and hell. The popular division is, however, called by the Hindus themselves, the *left-hand* Sakta faith. It is to this that the bloody sacrifices offered to Kali must be imputed ; and all the barbarities and indecencies perpetrated at the Durga Puja, the annual worship of Durga, and the Churuk Puja, the swinging festival, are to be ascribed. There are other atrocities which do not meet the public eye. This is not a random foundationless charge, we have the books describing the rites and ceremonies, some of them are in print, veiled necessarily in the obscurity of the original language, but incontrovertible witnesses of the veracity of the charge. Of course no respectable Hindu will admit that he is a Vamachari, a follower of the left-hand ritual, or that he is a member of a society in which meat is eaten, wine is drunk, and abominations not to be named are practised. The imputation will be indignantly denied, although, if the Tantras be believed, " many a man who calls himself a Saiva, or a Vaishnava, is secretly a Sakta, and a brother of the left-hand fraternity." *

The worshippers of Sakti have always been divided into two classes, a right and a left-hand order, and three sub-divisions of the latter were enumerated, who until lately were still well known —the Purnabhishiktas, Akritarthas, Kritakrityasamas.

Time, and the presence of foreign rulers, it is evident to all observers, have very much modified the character of much of the Hindu worship; if the licentious practices of the Saktas are still as prevalent as ever, which may well be questioned, they are, at least, carefully concealed from observation, and if they are not exploded, there are other observances of a more ferocious description, which seem to have disappeared. The worship of Bhairava, still prevails amongst the Saktas and the Jogis; but in upper India, at least, the naked mendicant, smeared with funeral ashes, armed with a trident or a sword, carrying a hollow skull in his hand, and half intoxicated with the spirits which he has quaffed from that disgusting wine-cup, prepared, in short, to perpetrate any act of violence and crime, the Kapalika of former days, is now rarely, if ever, encountered.

A hundred years ago, the worshippers of the Sakti were exceedingly numerous amongst all classes of Hindus, it was computed that of those of Bengal, at least three-fourths were of this sect. The bride of Siva in one or other of her many and varied forms, was by far the most popular emblem in Bengal, and along the Ganges.

The worship of the female principal, as distinct from the divinity, appears to have originated in the literal interpretation of the metaphorical language of the Vedas, in which the will or purpose to create the universe, is represented as originating from the creator, and co-existent with him as his bride, and part of himself. Thus in the Rig Veda, it is said, " That divine spirit breathed without afflation single, with her who is sustained within him; other than him nothing existed." First desire was formed in his mind, and that became the original productive seed, and the Sama

* Wilson's Lectures.

Veda, speaking of the divine cause of creation, says, "He felt not delight, being alone. He wished another, and instantly became such. He caused his ownself to fall in 'twain, and thus became husband and wife. He approached her, and thus were human beings produced. In those passages it is not unlikely that reference is made to the primitive tradition of the origin of mankind, but there is also a figurative representation of the first indication of wish or will in the Supreme Being. Being devoid of all qualities whatever, he was alone, until he permitted the wish to be multiplied to be generated with himself. This wish being put into action, it is said, became united with its parent, and then created beings were produced. Thus this first manifestation of divine power is termed *Ichchhárupaá*, personified desire, and the creator is designated as *Swechchamaya*, united with his own will; whilst in the Vedanta philosophy, and the popular sects, such as that of Kabir, and others, in which all created things are held to be illusory, the Sakti, or active will of the deity, is always designated and spoken of as Maya, or Mahamaya, original deceit or illusion.

CHAPTER VI.

Further account of Right-hand and Left-hand worship—The practices of the Vamis or Vamacharis—The rite of Mantra Sadhana—Ceremony of Sri Chakra—Claim of the priests to supernatural power—Legends.

WITH regard to what have been called right-hand and left-hand worship we proceed to develop a few further particulars on the authority of certain statements made in the Calcutta Review for 1848. When the worship of the Shakti is publicly performed, and in a manner quite harmonious to the Vaidik or Puranik ritual, and free from all obscene practices and impurities, it is termed the Dhakshina or right-hand form of worship; and those who adopt this pure ritual are termed Dhakshinacharis. The peculiarities of this sect were described at length, many years ago, in a work compiled by Kasinath, and entitled *Dhakshinachara, Tantra Raja*. According to this authority—the ritual declared in the Tantras of the Dhakshinacharis is pure, and conformable to the Vedas. Its leading parts are :—

1st.—*Auchmana*. The object of this, as well as some other ceremonies that follow, is the purification of the worshippers. It consists in taking up water from a copper vessel, with a small spoon of the same metal, by the left hand, and pouring a small quantity of it on the half-closed palm of the right hand : in sipping up this water thrice with the lips, and in touching with the fingers in rapid succession. the lips, the eyes, and other parts of the head, along with the repetition of proper formulæ. With respect to the quantity of water to be sipped, it is directed and strictly enjoined that it must be such as to run down the throat to the mouth of the œsophagus, and no further.

2nd.—*Shasti Buchana*. This part of the ceremony is performed with the view of rendering the result of adoration beneficial to the worshipper. Mention is now made of the month, the age of the moon, and the day in which the ceremony takes place, and then appropriate mantras are repeated, such as, like good omens, are believed to prognosticate happy results.

3rd.—*Sankalpa*. This is like the prayer part of a petition. In this the adorer discloses the immediate object of his worship, mentioning again by name the month, the fortnight, whether dark or bright, and the age of the moon. He mentions also his own proper name and his gotra, which is always the name of some rishi or saint. A fruit, generally a betel-nut or a *haretaki*, is necessary, which is held in the water contained in the copper vessel called Kosha.

4th.—*Ghatasthapana*, or the placing of a pot. This consists in placing a pot or jar, generally made of earth, but sometimes of brass or any pure metal, on a small elevation formed of mud,—the mud of the thrice sanctifying Ganges is of course preferable to any other. The jar is filled with water, a bunch of mango leaves, with a green cocoanut, or a ripe plantain, is placed on its top, and the sectarial mark called the yantra is painted with red lead on its front. This is to serve for a temporary abode of the goddess, whose presence in it is worshipfully solicited.

5th.—*Sámánya Argha Sthapana*. This part of the devotion is opened by offering prayers to the ten cardinal points, which, according to the Hindus, are the East, South-east, South, South-west, West, North-West, North, North-east, the Zenith, and the Nadir, presided over by Indra, Agni, Yama, Nairit, Baruna, Bayu, Kubera, Isha or Mohadeva, Brahma and Ananta. After this, what is called an Argha, composed of a small quantity of soaked rice and a few blades of durva-grass, is to be placed on a dumb conch-shell, on the left side of the worshipper; and if, besides the worshipper, any Brahman, or Brahmans be present, a few grains of rice must be given to each of them, after which, they all throw the rice on the pot.

6th.—*Ashan Suddhi*, or literally the purification of the seat, but technically, of the posture in which the worshipper is to sit or stand while engaged in his devotion. This varies according to the immediate object of worship. The Tantras prescribe eighty thousand different sorts of postures. Some of these are impossible, others are very painful, all are more or less ludicrous.

7th.—*Bhuta Shuddhi*, or the purification of the body. It is called Bhuta Suddhi, for the body is believed to be composed of the five elementary substances called bhuta, viz., earth, water, fire, air, and ether. In this observance, the worshipper is to conceive, that his old body is consumed, and that a new and purified one is put on. It is declared that fire and nectar are deposited in every man's forehead; and it is by this brain-fire that the old body is to be conceived to be reduced to ashes, on which nectar being mentally sprinkled over, a regenerated body must be conceived to come to existence by virtue of the mantras.

8th and 9th.—*Prándyáin* and *Rishyádinyás*. These are introductory prayers, inviting the presence of the goddess.

10th and 11th.—*Matrikanyas* and *Barnanyas*. These are singular rites, in which the worshipper repeats in order the letters of the Sanskrit alphabet, each with the Anaswara combined, as ang, áng, kang, khang, gang, ghang, and so on with the rest. And as he repeats these letters, which are fifty in number, he touches fifty different parts of his own body, according to directions minutely laid down in the Tantras; and when an earthen image of the goddess is to be worshipped for the first time, the officiating priest touches also the corresponding parts of the idol.

12th.—*Dyana*. In this, the worshipper is required, by closing both his eyes, to form the image of his guardian divinity in his mind, and to fix his mental vision upon it for some time.

13th.—*Abdhan, Chakshudán,* and *Pránpratisthá*. When the worship is performed without an image of the goddess, she is invoked to vouchsafe her presence in the jar.

14th.—*Pujah,* or the presenting of offerings of rice, fruit, incense, etc.

15th.—*Lelehi Mudra,* or the performance of the gesticulation called Lelehi, which consists in putting the palm of the right hand upon the back of the left, and shaking the fingers. There are no less than sixty-four thousand different sorts of Mudra prescribed in the Tantras.

16th.—*Abarana Pujah,* or the worship of the attendants of the goddess.

17th.—*Mahákála Pujah,* or the adoration of Mahákála, a form of Shiva.

18th.—*Balidan,* or the offering of sacrifice, commonly a blood offering.

19th.—*Kabajan Patheth*. In praise of the exploits of the goddess.

20th.—*Homa*. Pouring clarified butter upon the consecrated fire, made for the purpose on a bed of sand about one foot square. The ashes are worn on the forehead, and the residue carefully deposited or buried in a corner of the house.

The Vamis, or the left-hand worshippers, adopt a form of worship contrary to that which is usual, and they not only worship the Shakti of Siva in all her terrific forms, but pay adoration to her numerous fiend-like attendants, the Yoginis, Dakinis, and the Sankinis.

The rites practised by the Vamis or Vámácháris are so grossly obscene, as to cast into shade the worst inventions which the most impure imagination can conceive. "In this last mentioned sect (the Shaktas)," says a learned Sanskrit scholar, "as in most others, there is a right-handed and decent path, and a left-handed and indecent mode of worship, but the indecent worship of this sect is most grossly so, and consists of unbridled debauchery, with wine and women. This profligate sect is supposed to be numerous, though unavowed. In most parts of India, if not in all, they are held in deserved detestation ; and even the decent Shaktas do not make public profession of their tenets, nor wear on their foreheads the mark of the sect, lest they should be suspected of belonging to the other branch of it." Solitude and secrecy being strictly enjoined to the Vamis, they invariably celebrate their rites at midnight, and in most unfrequented and private places. They neither acknowledge their participation in these most scandalous orgies, nor, as we have already remarked, confess that they belong to any branch of the Shakta sect, although their reserve in this respect is becoming every day more and more relaxed, if not of all, at least, of many. Those, whose immediate object is the attainment of super-human powers, or whose end is specific, aiming at some particular boon or gift, are more strict on the point, lest they reap no fruits of their devotion. They never admit a companion, nor even one of their own fraternity, into the place of their worship. Even when they are believed by the credulous Hindus to have become Shiddas, that is, possessed of supernatural powers ; or in other words, when they have acquired sufficient art to impose upon their ignorant and superstitious countrymen, and have established their reputation as men capable of working miracles, they take every care not to disclose the means through which they have attained the object of their wishes, unless revealed by some accidental occurrence or unlooked-for circumstance. Those whose object is of a general character, hold a sort of convivial party, eating and drinking together in large numbers, without any great fear of detection. But yet they always take care to choose such secluded spots for the scenes of their devotion, as lie quite concealed from the public view. They generally pass unnoticed, and are traced out only when we make it our aim to detect them by watching over their movements like a spy. At present, as their chief desire appears to be only the gratification of sensual appetites, they are at all times found to be more attentive to points which have a direct reference to the indulgence of their favourite passions, than to those minor injunctions which require of them secrecy and solitude.

These, however, they are obliged to observe, at least in part, for their own account; for the abominations which, under the name of religious rites, they practice, cannot but expose them to disgrace and reproach, even among the degenerate Hindus.*

Guided by the same authority we present a brief summary of the principal rites observed by the above sect. The drinking of spirituous liquors, more or less, is with them, we are told, no less a habit than a religious practice. They will perform no religious ceremony without wine. In their various forms of daily worship, in the performance of all their ceremonial rites, in the celebration of all their public festivals, wine is indispensable. Every article of food which they offer to their goddess, is sprinkled over with the intoxicating liquor. Here it should be observed that the orthodox Vamis will never touch any foreign liquor or wine, but use only the country doasta, which they drink out of a cup formed either of the cocoa, or of a human skull. The liquor is first offered to their especial divinity in quart bottles or pints, but more frequently in *chaupalas* and earthen jars, and then distributed round the company, each member having a cup exclusively his own. If there be no company, the worshipper pours the liquor into his own cup and after certain motions and prayers, empties it at a single draught. They call themselves and all other men that drink wine, *birs* or heroes, and those that abstain from drinking, *pasus, i.e.*, beasts. No sooner is a child born, than they pour into its mouth a drop or two of wine; at the time of its Sankára, called the *Anna prásana*, which takes place at the sixth moon from its birth, if it be a male, or at the seventh moon, if it be a female, they give it pieces of cork or *shola* dipped in wine to be sucked, so they habituate the child from its cradle, in the drinking of spirituous liquors. At the time of the principal initiation, or *mantra grahana*, that is, when the specific or Bij mantra is received from the Guru, he and his new disciple drink together, the former at intervals giving instructions to the latter as to the proper mode of drinking. Whenever the spiritual guide visits a Kaula family, all its members, men, women, and children, gather round him, and with great cheers and feasting, drink his health as he drinks theirs. The fact is, drinking is carried on to an infamous and degrading extent, their principle is said to be, drink, and drink, and drink again, till you fall flat on the ground; the moment you rise, drink again, and you shall obtain final liberation.

---

* Religious Sects of India by H. H. Wilson.

In justice to some who are exceptions to this rule, we must observe that all Vámácháris are not drunkards, though they all drink. Some of the Tantras prescribe the exact quantity to be drunk. According to their prescription, the least dose to be taken is an ounce, and the largest not exceeding three ounces.

There is another variety of the Vámis who substitute certain mixtures in the place of wine. These mixtures are declared in the Tantras to be equivalent to wine, and to possess all its intrinsic virtues without the power of intoxication; such as the juice of the cocoanut received in a vessel made *kansa*: the juice of the watermelon mixed with sugar, and exposed to the sun; molasses dissolved in water, and contained in a copper vessel, etc.

In all the ceremonies, which not only comprehend the worship of the Shakti, but are performed for the attainment of some proposed object, the presence of a female, as the living representative, and the type of the goddess, is indispensably necessary. Such ceremonies are specific in their nature, and are called *Shádhanás*. Some who are more decent than the rest of the sect, join their wives in the celebration of the gloomy rites of Kali. Others make their beloved mistresses partners in their joint devotion. Here the rite assumes a blacker aspect. The favourite concubine is disrobed, and placed by the side or on the thigh of her paramour who is in the same condition. In this situation, the usual calmness of the mind must be preserved, and no evil lodged in it. Such is the requisition of the Shastras, say the Vámis, when reproached for their brutal practices.

In this way is performed the rite called the *Mantra Sádhaná*. It is, as must be expected, carried on in great secrecy, and is said to lead to the possession of supernatural powers. The religious part of it is very simple, consisting merely of the repetition of the Mula mantra, which may or may not be preceded by the usual mode of Shakta worship. Hence it is called the *Mantra Sádhaná*, to distinguish it from other sorts of Sádhanás. After ten P.M., the devotee, under pretence of going to bed, retires into a private chamber, where, calling his wife or mistress, and procuring all the necessary articles of worship, such as wine, grains, water, a string of beads, etc., he shuts the doors and the windows of the room, and, sitting before a lighted lamp, joins with his partner in drinking. The use of this preliminary is obvious. When, by the power of the spirits, the veil of shame is withdrawn, he, making his wife or mistress sit in the manner already described, begins to repeat his mantra, and continues to do so till one, two, or three o'clock in the morning. At intervals the glass is repeated, and the ceremony is closed in a manner which decency does not allow us to state.

We now come to the blackest part of the Vámá worship. Nothing can be more disgusting, nothing more abominable, nothing more scandalously obscene, than the rite we are about to describe. The ceremony is called Shi-Chakra, Purnábhisheka, the ring or full initiation. This worship is mostly celebrated in mixed societies, composed of motley groups of various castes, though not of creed. This is quite extraordinary, since, according to the established laws of the caste system, no Hindu is permitted to eat with an inferior. But here the rule is at once done away with, and persons of high caste, low caste, and no caste, sit, eat, and drink together. This is authorised by the Shastras in the following text :—" While the Bhairavi Tantra (the ceremony of the Chakra) is proceeding, all castes are Brahmans—when it is concluded they are again distinct." Thus while the votaries of the Shakti observe all the distinctions of caste in public, they neglect them altogether in the performance of her orgies.

The principal part of the rite called the Chakra is Shakti Sádhaná or the purification of the female representing the Shakti. In the ceremony termed mantra Sádhaná, we have already noticed the introduction of a female, the devotee always making his wife or mistress partner in his devotion. This cannot be done in a mixed society. For although the Vámis are so far degenerated as to perform rites such as human nature, corrupt as it is, revolts from with detestation, yet they have not sunk to that depth of depravity as to give up their wives to the licentiousness of men of beastly conduct. Neither is it the ordination of the Shastras. For this purpose they prescribe females of of various descriptions, particularly " a dancing girl, a female devotee, a harlot, a washerwoman, or barber's wife, a female of the Braminical or Sudra tribe, a flower girl, or a milk maid." Some of the Tantras add a few more to the list, such as a princess, the wife of a Kápali, or of a Chandal, of a Kulála, or of a conch seller. Others increase the number to twenty-six, and a few even to sixty-four. These females are distinguished by the name of Kula Shakti. Selecting and procuring females from the preceding classes, the Vamacharis are to assemble at midnight in some sequestered spot, in eight, nine, or eleven couples, the men representing Bhairavas or Viras, and the women Bhairavas or Náyikás. In some cases a single female personating the Shakti is to be procured. In all cases, the Kula Shakti is placed disrobed, but richly adorned with ornaments on the left of a circle (chakra) described for the purpose, whence the ceremony derives its name. Sometimes she is made to stand, totally destitute of clothing, with protuberent tongue and dishevelled hair. She is then purified by the recitation of many mantras and texts, and by the performance of the mudra or gesticulations. Finally she is sprinkled over with wine, and if not previously initiated, the Bij mantra is thrice repeated in her ear. To this succeeds the worship of the guardian divinity; and after this, that of the female, to whom are now offered broiled fish, flesh, fried peas, rice, spirituous liquors, sweetmeats, flowers, and other offerings, which are all purified by the repeating of incantations and the sprinkling of wine. It is now left to her choice to partake of the offerings, or to rest contented simply with verbal worship. Most frequently she eats and drinks till she is perfectly satisfied, and the refuse is shared by the persons present. If, in any case, she refuses to touch or try either meat or wine, her worshippers pour wine on her tongue while standing, and receive it as it runs down her body in a vessel held below. This wine is sprinkled over all the dishes which are now served among the votaries.

Such is the preliminary called the purification of the Shakti. To this succeds the devotional part of the ceremony. The devotees are now to repeat their radical mantra, but in a manner unutterably obscene. Then follow things too abominable to enter the ears of men, or to be borne by the feelings of an enlightened community; things, from which the rudest savage would turn away his face with disgust.

* * * * * *

Here the diabolical business closes.

The religious practices of the Shaktas being such as are believed to lead to the possession of supernatural powers, many persons of this sect, taking advantage of the religious blunders of the great mass of the people, practice the most barefaced impositions. The credulity of the Hindus becomes to many an inexhaustible source of wealth, especially to those who are at the head of any religious establishment, where any form of the Shakti is the presiding divinity. These priests who day and night attend on the goddess, and perform various mystical rites, gradually acquire the credit of having close intimacy and secret communication with her; and then gifts, presents, and votive offerings are incessantly poured on the altar. Under pretence of healing diseases of children, and curing barrenness, mothers and young women are induced to join in the worship of Kali, when the worthy votaries of the black goddess, the priests, thank her for having fulfilled the object of their wishes. Offerings are presented, not only for receiving blessings, but also for personal safety. Life and death are said to be in the hands of these Shiddhas. They, if provoked, can sooner or later, kill the offender by the power of their mantras. This deadly ceremony is called Máranuchchátan. There is in one district, a temple dedicated to Shiddheswari, a form of Kali, the late attending priest of which was a man universally believed to be of no common rate. The belief yet prevails in the neighbourhood, that once in the height of indignation he caused the death of a rich native for having indirectly called him a drunkard. The story runs thus :—At a feast given to the Brahmans by this native gentleman, the priest of Shiddheswari was invited to his house,—the latter, on account of the manifold duties of the temple, was late in his attendance, on which the host, being displeased with his conduct, said to him as he entered the door, " Well, Bhattacharjya, now I believe the dimness of your eyes has vanished," alluding to his known habit of drinking. At this raillery, the rage of the favourite of Kali knew no bounds. He instantly returned to the temple and closed its doors, strictly enjoining his servants not to disturb his meditation before flames from the funeral pile of the wretched host ascended to the skies. And, wonderful to relate, an hour had scarcely elapsed, before the sons of the host came to the priest with clothes around their necks, fell suppliant on their knees, and with folded hands implored his mercy, saying, " O ! Sir, save us and our family." The priest smiling, asked them what was the matter, to which they replied, weeping, " Our father is no more. No sooner had your holy feet left our doors, than on a sudden blood came out rushing from his mouth, he fell on the ground and expired. Save us, we entreat thee, and the rest of his family, for we have not offended against thy holy divinity." On this, the wrath of the priest was pacified, and he spoke to them in an affectionate tone ; " No fear, my children, you are safe, go home and perform your father's funeral obsequies."

Another marvellous anecdote is told of him, as well as of many others of similar character. When on one occasion he was bringing liquor concealed in a water-pot, a person whose object was to expose him, stopped him on the way and wanted to see what was in the pot. To this he calmly replied, nothing but milk. Saying this, he poured out the contents, and the liquor was found converted into milk. Such persons, by taking advantage of the fears of the superstitious Hindus, extort money and other presents from them.

Much of the splendour of the Hindu idolatry consists in the celebration of the Shakta rites. The great festivals, which are annually celebrated in Bengal, such as the Durga Puja, the Jagaddhari and Kali Pujas, the Charak, the Basanti, Rutanti and Falahari Pujas, are all Shaktya observances, and for the most part performed by the worshippers of the Shakti. These festivals themselves, and the exhibitions that accompany them, exert a pernicious influence over the morals of the people. The spirit in which these religious days are kept, the splendid and fascinating ceremonies connected with them, and the merry exhibitions, including savage music and indecent dancing, that form a part of the worship, cannot but captivate and corrupt the heart and overpower the judgment of youth.

The Shakta processions are utterly abominable. One of them takes place after the blood-offerings at public festivals. Of a similar character are those which go before and follow the images, when carried to be thrown into the river or into a pond. On these occasions the Shaktas utter terms most grossly obscene, loudly and repeatedly, and make gestures the most indecent that can be imagined ; and all this before their goddess and the public.

The habit of drinking wine, which prevails so widely among the Shaktas, produces baneful effects on the minds of the Hindus. Leaving the Kaulas as out of the question, since they themselves train up their children in the habit of drinking, the Shaktas in general are more forward in trying the qualities of the prohibited article than any other sect of the orthodox Hindus, and their example stimulates others to do the same. This is one of the reasons why the drinking of spirituous liquors, which was almost unknown among the Hindus of yore, has gradually become so prevalent among them, as at this day. The tenets of the Shaktas open the way for the gratification of all the sensual appetites, they hold out encouragement to drunkards, thieves and dacoits ; they present the means of satisfying every lustful desire ; they blunt the feelings by authorising the most cruel practices, and lead men to commit abominations which place them on a level with the beasts. The Shaktya worship is impure in itself, obscene in its practices, and highly injurious to the life and character of men.*

* See Calcutta Review for 1855.

CHAPTER VII.

Considerations respecting the origin of Phallic worship—Comparisons between Indian and Egyptian practices and doctrines.

FOR the bulk of the evidence respecting Phallic or Nature Worship, and for illustrations of its original character and ultimate developments, it is evident that India is the land to which we must chiefly look for information: for this reason the majority of the preceding pages deal with that part of the world. Historically perhaps there is considerable difficulty in deciding as to where this worship originated; its antiquity is so great, and its diffusion throughout various countries so general and extensive, that it appears impossible to say whether Greece, Rome, India, or Egypt was its earliest home or birthplace.

There are some considerations, however, which render it probable that it was in India where its earliest manifestations were exhibited. Whatever impurities and abominations may have clustered round it in comparatively modern times, the fact must not be lost sight of, that in its earlier phases in that country nothing was associated with it that was calculated to cause any offence to the most refined and modest of minds. Very little judgment is needed to understand that the tendency of practices thus appealing to the most easily excited of the animal passions would be downward rather than upward, that instead of growing pure and free from the taint of lustful desires, the almost inevitable fruit would be impurity and licentious indulgence; it is not likely therefore that the more respectable worship of early India would be the product of the gross practices of the other nations we have named. We can see clearly enough, we think, the origin of this worship resting upon the highest aspirations of the human soul. In endeavouring to frame a theological system and arrange a method of worship to meet the cravings of the mind for intercourse with the creative powers of the universe, men would be sure to fix their thoughts upon those means and agents by which living beings and things were brought into existence, and which, to say the least of it, acted as secondary causes in the creative work. These, of course, would be the generative organs of men and animals in general, and for want of better and more exalted teaching, they would easily enough persuade themselves that it was a proper thing to worship the power symbolized by such objects, if they did not actually worship the objects themselves. Perhaps originally, the first of these two ideas was all that was intended or contemplated, for it is undeniable that many cases have come under our notice in which men were really rendering adoration to an unknown spiritual power when they appeared to be doing nothing but worshipping a graven image.

There is no doubt the religious system of the Hindus is very ancient, and it has been supposed by some that it was formed about the same time as that of the Egyptians, from which that of the Greeks and other western nations was in some measure derived. Many points of resemblance have been observed between them, too many, and too striking, to have been fortuitous. Even some of the inhabitants of Ethiopia appear to have been of the same origin with those of Hindostan, and both the Ethiopians and Egyptains seem to have had some connection or intercourse with the Hindoos; but of what kind it was, or when it subsisted, we have no certain account; and they appear to have been so long separated, that at present they are in total ignorance of each other.

According to Eusebius and Syncellus, some people from the river Indus settled in the neighbourhood of Egypt in the reign of Amenophis, the father of Sesostris, and many Egyptians, banished by their princes, settled in other countries and went as far as India. It is also supposed that many of the priests of Egypt left the country on the invasion of it by Cambyses. But such circumstances as these are not sufficient to account for the great resemblance between the two systems. The Hindoos themselves say that their sacred books came from the West, but they themselves, no doubt, as well as their books, came from that quarter, and their sacred books, it is supposed, were probably composed while the seat of the empire was in Persia.

There are a few Egyptain words similar to those in the ancient language of Hindostan, which seem to shew that the two people had some affinity to each other. *Brama*, pronounced *birouma* in Malabar, signifies man, and so did *pirouma* in the language of Egypt. The name of the river of Egypt, Nile, is probably Sanscrit, since *nila* in that language, signifies blue, and the ancients say it had its name from that colour.

But circumstances of much more importance than these discover some early connection between Hindostan and Egypt. The names and figures of the twelve signs of the Zodiac among the

Hindoos are nearly the same with ours, which came from Egypt through Greece, and each of these signs is divided into thirty degrees. Both the Egyptians and Hindoos had also the same division of time into weeks, and they denominated each of the days by the names of the same planets.

The resemblance between the Oriental and Occidental systems extends much farther than Egypt. The office and power of the Druids in the northern parts of Europe, did not differ much from those of the Bramins; and the Etruscans, from whom the Romans derived the greatest part of their learning and religion, had a system which had a near affinity with that of the Persians and Indians, and they wrote alternately to the right hand and the left.

Several remarkable general principles were held alike by the ancient Egyptians and the Hindoos. They both believed that the souls of men existed in a prior state, and went into other bodies after death. They had the same ideas of the body being a prison to the soul, and imagined that they could purify and exalt the soul by the mortification of the body; and from the idea of the great superiority of spiritual to corporeal substances, they held all *matter* in great contempt. They also believed (according to La Croze) that plants had a principle of animation.

Several religious ideas and customs were common to both countries. The Egyptians of Thebais represented the world under the figure of an egg, which came from the mouth of Cneph, and this resembled the first production according to the Hindoo system. Several of the Egyptian deities were both male and female, which corresponds with the figure of the lingam with the Hindoos. This obscene figure, at least the phallus, was much used in the Egyptian worship, and from Egypt it was carried into Greece, where it was used in the mysteries of Bacchus. As the Hindoos worshipped their god Siva under this figure, and carried it in procession, the Egyptians and Greeks did the same with the phallus. Also, the lascivious postures of the Egyptian women before their god Apis, were the same as those of the Hindoo women before their idols. The Hindoos also chose their sacred bulls by the same marks as were used by the Egyptians.

Then, again, the account of the flight of the Egyptian gods, as given by the Greeks, and their concealing themselves under the forms of animals, bears some resemblance to the various transformations of Vishnu. Also, the Egyptians worshipped the Nile and the Hindoos the Ganges. Some of the Hindoo temples have the same remarkable form, viz., that if a pyramid, or cone. That the

PHALLIC MISCELLANIES.   91

pyramids of Egypt had some religious use can hardly be doubted. All the pagodas are in that form, or have towers of that form in the buildings which surround them. The temples in Pegu are also of a conical form. Sir William Jones says that the pyramids of Egypt, as well as those discovered in Ireland, and probably also the tower of Babel, seem to have been intended for images of Mahadeva, or Siva. One other thing, the onion, which was held in veneration by the Egyptians, is not eaten by the Hindoos.

Not only do we find the same general principles, and the same, or similar, religious customs, but some of the same gods among the Hindoos, Egyptians, and Greeks. The Egyptian Cneph was the Supreme intelligence, which was never lost sight of by the Hindoos. With the Egyptians, Isis represented not only the moon, but sometimes the powers of Nature, which were supposed to have been in a great measure derived from the moon; and in Bengal and Japan, also, the same is called Isari, or Isi, and is described as a goddess with many arms. According to Sir William Jones, Iswara of the Hindoos is the Osiris of the Egyptians, and Nared, a distinguished son of Brahma, resembles Hermes, or Mercury. A statute of Jupiter had a third eye in its forehead, and Siva has three eyes. Diodorus Siculus and Plutarch say that Osiris signifies a person that has many eyes, and Siva is drawn with an additional eye in his forehead, though the phallus is his usual form. Osiris was said to have been killed by Typhon, and Chib cut off the head of Brahma.

Indra of the Hindoos, called also Divespiter, is Jupiter, or Diespiter; the bull of Iswara is the Apis, or Ap, of Egypt. Cartraya, with six faces and many eyes, was the Egyptian Orus, and the Mars of Italy. Sri, or Iris, called also Pedna, and Camala, was Ceres, and according to Herodotus, she was the Egyptian Isis. Ganesu was Janus. Visuacarman, the Indian forger of arms for the gods, was Vulcan. The Rama of India is Dyonisus, called also Bromius by the Greeks: Krishnu or Vishnu, is Apollo, and in Irish, it signifies the sun. According to the Vedas and other sacred works, a bad genius, or giant, seizes on the sun and moon when they are eclipsed, and the Egyptians ascribed the same thing to their Typhon, who was said even to have swallowed their god Horus, or the Sun.

The Egyptians at certain festivals carried the images of their gods in procession. Herodotus says they drew one of them in a carriage with four wheels, and the same was done by the Hindoos. The Egyptians held cows in much greater veneration than any other animals; they were sacred to Isis, and never sacrificed. Some superstitious respect was also paid to horned cattle by the Persians. In an account of the Zendavesta, Ormusd, the Supreme Being, directs Zerdusht to render worship and praise to the *Supreme Ox*, and to the rain, of which the angel Jashter, who subsists in the form of an ox, is the distributor. The Hindoos made some use of the image of a bull, as Mr. Sonnerat relates in his account of some of their Temples, though they never carried their superstition in this respect so far as the Egyptians, who made live bulls the immediate objects of their worship.

It may be said that in all this there is a great deal of mere conjecture, and therefore of uncertainty; the evidence, however, upon which it is founded, coming from a number of independent scources from writers of repute, learning, and veracity—is not easily disposed of. It seems conclusive that systems very like one another indeed prevailed in different parts of the world, and though similar situations may lead to similar sentiments, and corresponding practices, the above mentioned similarity is too great, and extends to too many particulars, to be thus accounted for. It is not at all extraordinary that men who had no communication with each other should be equally worshippers of the sun, moon, and stars, that they should fancy deep caverns, or thick woods, to be haunted with spirits, that particular rivers should have their several genii, or deities dispensing their waters at their pleasure, as the sun, they might suppose, did his heat, and the moon, the stars, and the planets their peculiar influences; but that they should adopt the same rites in the worship of these natural deities, and especially that they should give them *attributes*, and even *names*, so nearly alike, is beyond the effect of accident.

The conclusion we come to, and which we think is fully warranted by all the circumstances, is, that the great mass of phallic worship existing in different parts of the world began in India, and gradually found its way into the western nations, becoming, as was perfectly natural with such a system, more and more depraved as time went on, and as it was found that it could be made subservient to the desires and passions of licentious men,

Our frontispiece represents a pious female propitiating Mahadeva or Siva in his generative character, indicated by the Linga, inserted in its appropriate receptacle, the Argha, or Yoni. The engraving is taken from a picture which Moor describes as being delicately executed, the female being young, handsome, and elegantly dressed. She is performing the ceremony of *Linga puja*, to which such frequent references is made in these pages, and she has spread out in front of her the various objects required in that service. The symbol is placed in one of the many domestic temples, common at one time in India, known as Dewal, or Devel, from Deva, a *deity*, and *havela*, a house, literally a house of God. It is this erection which is ordinarily written pagoda, by the English, a word not used in India. The stone of the building is white, its lines gold, and it is surmounted by a gold spire, called Sekra; when temples, or other things have a conical, or pine-apple shaped termination, such ornament is called Kalasa. The exterior of the temple is white, its interior, ash coloured, like its patron deity, the Linga and Asgha are of black stone with gilt edges : the Linga (the upright conical stone), which has mystical orange coloured lines traced on it, is crowned with encircled folds of Bilva flowers; and a chaplet of three strings of them, white with yellow buds at regular distances, hangs pendent from the top of the Linga, falling towards the termination or spout of the Argha. The Bilva is a shrub consecrated to Mahadeva, who alone wears a chaplet of its flowers, which are offered in sacrifice to no other deity. The various implements used in the puja to Siva are, five lighted lamps; (or one lamp with five wicks) a spouted vessel holding lustral water; a cup for ghee; another cup for water with which to sprinkle the flowers; and a bell rung at certain times to scare away evil spirits.

The woman sits on an embroidered carpet, called Asana : her right hand is in a bag of gold brocade, the hand being supposed to hold a rosary of round beads, 108 in number without the connecting ones.

This picture admirably illustrates the true character of the original lingam-worship of India, and fully bears out all that has been said respecting its original freedom from the indecencies which afterwards became so flagrant and universal.

CHAPTER VIII.

Vocabulary of words of Indian and Sanscrit origin.

Abádi—An inhabited place.
Aban—The name of the eighth month.
Abáshan.—A low caste of labourers.
Abd—A slave.
Abdáli—Fakirs of the báshara order.
Abdár—A servant who prepares water for domestic use.
Abdhut—A sect of religious mendicants.
Abhir—A caste employed as cowherds and shepherds.
Abkár—A maker of strong waters.
Abri—A building stone found at Kabul.
Achárgya—A caste of Bengalese, said to have originated from the Brahmins.
Achárya—A teacher.
Achátur—A caste of cultivators of the soil.
Adálat—A court of justice.
Adar—The ninth month.
Adbhutásánti—A burnt sacrifice used to counteract evil omens.
Adhipati—A ruler.
Adhwaryu—The third class of priests employed at a vedic sacrifice.
Adi Granth—The chief scripture of the Sikhs.
Adináth—The first arhat of the Jains.
Aditya—The sun.
Adlingadawar—A caste of agriculturists.
Advichinchi—A caste of cultivators of the land.
Afrit—A demon.
Agarwala—A trading caste.
Agasa—A caste of washermen.
Aghora—Religious mendicants who sometimes feed on human flesh.
Agiari—A temple in which perpetual fire is maintained.
Agni—The god of fire.
Aguri—A Bengalese caste of cultivators.
Ahri—One of the Himalayan gods.
Ahriman—The personification of evil in the Zoroastrian religion.

Akshamala—A string of beads.
Alifshai—The Benawa fakirs.
Amanth—A Bengalese caste employed as servants.
Amaras—Immortal.
Ambattan—A caste employed as barbers.
Amma Kodagas—A sect driven away by the Brahmins.
Anant—Endless, a name applied to Vishnu and other gods.
Andhyaru—A Parsi priest.
Andra—A Buddhist dynasty considered to have reigned in India from 31 B.C. to 429 A.D.
Anila—The god of fire.
Annapurná—The goddess who is said to feed the inhabitants of Benares.
Aranyaka—A part of the Veda, considered so holy that it may be read only in the solitude of a forest.
Archáka—An officiating priest at a pagoda.
Ardha-matra—A mysterious word applicable to the deity.
Ardhanárisa—Name of Siva in his form as half male, half female.
Arjà—A female mendicant.
Asani—A small seat, also a carpet used at prayers.
Asiloma—A demon who had swords instead of hair.
Asthal—A temple.
Asura—A spirit.
Atasil—The eight precepts binding on an upasaka.
Atharwa—The name of the fourth veda.
Aukamma—A village goddess.
Avasta—The Zoroastrian scriptures.
Ayenar—A god of India who is supposed to guard the fields from demons.
Azád—An order of fakirs.

Bagh—A garden.
Bahucharaji—A goddess worshipped in Gujarat.
Bahuta—An amulet worn on the arm by the worshippers of Narsingh.
Bai—A lady.
Baidni—A woman of the Baidya caste.
Baidya—A caste supposed to be the offspring of a Brahman father and Vaisya mother.
Baláí—A caste of Sudras.
Balarám—The elder brother of Krishna, sometimes an incarnation of Vishnu.

Bána—An arrow.
Bandhá—A slave or bondmen.
Baráhan—A goddess who is supposed to cure swelled hands and feet.
Barát—The final ceremony of a marriage.
Barwa—A wise man of the Bhils.
Basani—A prostitute, or female dedicated to a god.
Basawa—The sacred bull.
Báshkala—A demon.
Benawa—A community of fakirs of the beshara order.
Beshara—Those fakirs who hold themselves above the law.
Bhadarià—Mendicant astrologers of Brahman origin.
Bhadu—A low class of Uriya Brahmans.
Bhagat—A worshipper.
Bhagván—The divine spirit.
Bhagwat—A name for God.
Bhairawa—A name of Sivr.
Bhairawanath—A name of Siva.
Bhairon—*same as* Bhaironath.
Bhákta—A devotee.
Bhávin—A woman devoted to the service of the Temple.
Bhikhu—A religious mendicant.
Bhopi—A priest of a village temple.
Bhu—The earth.
Bhut—The spirit of the dead; a goblin.
Bhuteswara—A name of Siva as destroyer.
Bhutya—Devotees of Bhawani.
Bilwa—The bel tree.
Bisheswar—A name of Siva, alluding to his having swallowed poison.
Boa—A Temple.
Bo-tree—The pipal.
Brahmá—The Creator.
Bráhman—The first of the Hindu castes.
Bráhmáni—A woman of Brahman caste.
Broto—A vow.
Budibudaki—A religious beggar who smears himself with ashes.
Burha-Deo—The great God.
But—The name of a devi.

Catanar—A priest of the Syrian Church.
Chakra—The weapon of Vishnu.
Chattur—A consecrated cake of cow-dung.

Chhandas—A sacred hymn.
Chhandoga—A name of the udgatri priest.
Chillah—A forty days' fast.
Chitpáwan—A subdivision of the Maharashtra Brahmans.
Chitragupta—The first of the ministers of Yama.
Cholipanth—A sect of Panjabis allowing free sexual intercourse.
Chori—A marriage hall.
Churel—A hobgoblin in the form of a hideous woman.
Crore—Ten millions.

Dádá—An elderly person, or a paternal grandfather.
Dádupanthi—A Vaishnawa sect founded by Dadu.
Daftar—A register.
Dágoba—A dome-like structure built over the relics of a saint.
Dáin—A witch.
Daitya—A demon.
Daiwatapka—Parsi betrothal ceremony.
Dakaut—Braminical astrological mendicants.
Dakiri—A female imp who feeds upon human flesh.
Dachocha—A caste said to be descended from a Brahman father and a Gauli mother.
Dakshina—A cow fit to be given to a Brahman.
Danawa—A demon.
Dargah—The tomb of a saint.
Dasi—A woman dedicated to a temple.
Dastur—A Parsi high priest.
Devi—A goddess; especially Durga.
Devrukhi—The room of a temple where the idol stands.
Dewa—A god.
Dewánga—One who wears the emblem of Siva.
Dewasthán—A temple.
Dewatá—A deity.
Dhumra—A giant.
Dinesha—Lord of the day.
Diwar—Divinity of a village, for whom a portion of the grain is set apart at each harvest.
Dobe—A brahma who has studied two of the four Vedas.
Durdhara—A leader in the army of demons.
Durgá—The consort of Siva.
Durgá-pugá—The worship of Durgá.
Durmukha—The name of a demon—the fury faced.
Dwáparayuga—The Third age of the world.

Eshana—One of the names of Siva.

Fakir—A Mohommedan religious mendicant.

Gábhára—The inner room of a temple where the idol stands.
Gadipati—Chief of a body of religious mendicants.
Ganesa—A god, the son of Siva.
Garudi—A snake charmer.
Gentoo—Another name for a Hindu.
Ghaus—E fakir of the highest sanctity.
Gomedha—The sacrifice of a cow.
Gondhal—A noisy festival in honour of Devi.
Gopura—Building over the gate of a temple.
Gorakhnath—A name of Siva.
Gosain—An ascetic.
Goshanashin—A Mohomedan ascetic.
Grámadewatá—Tutelary deity of a village.
Granthi—A reader of the Granth, or Sikh Scriptures.
Grihadava—The tutelary god of a house.
Grihastha—A Brahman in the second asrama.
Guga—A saint to whom offerings are made to avert danger from snakes.
Guru—A religious teacher.

Haj—A pilgrimage.
Haji—One who has performed the Haj.
Hambali—One of the orthodox schools of Sunnis.
Har—A name of Siva.
Hara—The destroyer.
Harpuji—The worship of the plough.
Homa—An oblation made by pouring butter on a fire.
Hotri—The highest class of priest employed at a Vedic sacrifice.
Huttari—Festival in honour of the rice harvest.

Id-al-fitr—Festival of breaking fast.
Idgáh—A place of prayer for Mussalmans.
Imám—The officiating priest of a mosque.
Indra—The king of the firmament.
Iravata—The elephant of Indra.
Ishna-namaz—Prayer of sunset.
Ishrak-namaz—Prayer at sunrise.
Ishtadewa—A favourite deity.
Iswara—A name of Siva.

Ját—A vigil kept by Sudras on the tenth night after a sudden death, in order to summon the spirit of the deceased into the body of his son, or other person, and reveal the cause of death, the place where his treasures are hidden, or other matter desired to be known.—*J. T. Molesworth.*
Jagannáth—A name of Vishnu.
Jajmán—A patron.
Janárdan—A name of Vishnu.
Jánhavi—A name of the Ganges.
Játra—A pilgrimage to a holy place.
Jin—A goblin.
Jivagár—A Buddhist ascetic.
Jnándewa-panthi—A supposed incarnation of Vishnu.

Kabir-panthi—A Vaishnawa sect, followers of Kabir.
Kailása—The heaven of Siva.
Káli—The wife of Siva.
Kalki—The name of Vishnu in his tenth awatar, which is to take place at the end of the present, or kali, age, when he will destroy the wicked and inaugurate a new age of purity.—*Whitworth.*
Karniji—A goddess worshipped in Bikaner.
Kátáyani—A name of the goddess Parvati.
Kesari—The name of the lion of Durga.
Keshava—One of the names of Vishnu.
Khatib—The preacher in the mosque on Fridays and feast-days.
Khirakasi—A sect of Hindus who renounced idolatry and Brahmanism.
Khodiár—The devi of one of seven sisters of the Charan caste.
Koti—A crore, or ten millions.
Kowmári—A appellation of Durga.
Kowshiki—A goddess that emanated from Párvati.
Kuber—The god of riches.

Lakshmi—Wife of Vishnu.
Linga—The phallus or emblematic representation of Siva.
Lingait—A sect of Saiwas who wear the emblem of the linga.
Lohana—The most numerous class of Hindus in Sindh.
Lokas—The world.

Madhu—The name of a demon.
Madhwáchárya—A Vaishava sect.
Mahádeva—A name of Siva.

Mahájanwádi—A place were caste feasts are celebrated.
Mahákála—A name of Siva.
Mahéswar—A name of Siva.
Mánbhawa—A Vaishnava sect.
Mantra—Form of worship in the oldest part of the veda.
Manu—Man. Founder of the Manvantara.
Máruta—Wind. A god of the wind.
Masjid—A Mohommedan church.
Mastán—The Rasulsháhi fakirs.
Mátá—Name applied to various goddesses.
Matiá—A believer.
Matsya—The first principal awater of Vishnu.
Mobed—A Parsi priest.
Mund—A demon.
Muni—A saint.
Mundphoda—The Gurzmar fakirs, who beat their heads until they bleed in order to extort charity.
Musá Sohág—A body of fakirs who dress as women.
Mutawalli—The warden of a mosque.

Nádiyá—A bull marked as sacred.
Nágá—Naked.
Nágéswaraswámi—A serpent deity.
Nama—A mark worn on the forehead by followers of Vishnu.
Námadári—A Vaishnava.
Nandana—A beautiful garden in Indra's heaven.
Nandá Devi—A name of Durga.
Nandi—Siva's bull.
Narak—The place of punishment for souls.
Narakásur—A demon son of Bhumi, slain by Vishnu.
Narangkár—The maker of men.
Náráyana—The divine spirit moving on the waters.
Narsinh—A form assumed by Vishnu in order to destroy the demon Hiranyakásipu.
Nat—A spirit supposed to have the power to ward off evil.
Navar—A Parsi priest of low order.
Nazar—The evil eye.
Nimbárka—A Vaishavan sect worshipping Krishna and Radha conjointly.
Nirwána—Having the fire of life extinguished.

Pagoda—A Hindu temple in the south of India.

Parameshvari—A name of Durga.
Paramahansa—A sect of Siva's devotees.
Pariah—An outcast from society.
Párvati—The consort of Siva.
Pasupati—A name of Siva.
Pátála—The nether regions.
Pávaka—The god of fire.
Pináki—A name of Siva.
Prakriti—A goddess.
Pundarikaksha—Lotus-eyed.
Purusha—Man; the human soul.

Rájasuya—A sacrifice performed at a coronation.
Rali—The deified spirit of a woman who drowned herself on being married to a child.
Rámánandi—A sect of Vaisnavas.
Rámánuja—A Vaishawan sect in the south of India.
Ramban—A priest of high rank.
Rath—A war chariot.
Rig—The first Veda.
Rishi—A sage or hermit.
Rozah—A fast.
Rudra—The storm-god.

Sádhu—A saint.
Sadrá—The sacred shirt worn by the Parsis.
Sadubá—The name of a goddess.
Sákta—A worshipper of a sakti.
Sakti—Power.
Sama—The third Veda.
Sanhita—A collection of Vedic hymns.
Sannyási—An ascetic.
Saptapadi—Seven steps taken round the sacred fire, part of a Hindu marriage.
Saravasti—Goddess of eloquence and literature.
Sastri—A teacher.
Sattra—A sacrifice.
Sanra—A worshipper of the sun.
Sávitri—One of the incarnations of Sarasvati.
Shakra—One of the denominations of Indra.
Shakti—Power.
Shambu—An appellation of Siva.

Siva—The third person of the Hindu triad.
Srawak—A Buddhist saint.
Sura—A deity.

Tarpana—Offering of water.
Trinetra—Three-eyed.

Ugni—God of fire.
Umbiká—A name of Durga.

Vaishnavi—The consort of Vishnu.
Vanhi—One of the names of the god of fire.
Vidhi—One of the names of Brahma.
Vipra—A person who recites Vedas.
Vishnu—The second person of the Hindu triad, the preserver.
Vrutra—The name of a demon.

Yogini—A class of malicious female fiends.

Nature Worship and Mystical Series.

Cr. 8vo, Vellum, 7s. 6d. each, nett.

Only a very limited number, PRIVATELY PRINTED.

PHALLICISM.—A Description of the Worship of **Lingam-Yoni** in various parts of the World, and in different Ages, with an Account of Ancient and Modern Crosses, particularly of the **Crux Ansata** (or Handled Cross) and other Symbols connected with the Mysteries of **Sex Worship.** (*Only in sets*), *or* 10s. 6d. *separately.*

The importance of this subject, may be gleaned from the following remarks of Major Gen. Forlong. "Our Queen rules over, according to the latest census returns, some 100 millions of PURE-PHALLIC worshippers, that is three times the population of these Islands, and if we say merely Phallo-Solar worshippers, then 200 millions."

OPHIOLATREIA.—An Account of the Rites and Mysteries connected with the Origin, Rise, and Development of **Serpent Worship** in various parts of the World, enriched with Interesting Traditions, and a full description of the celebrated Serpent Mounds and Temples, the whole forming an exposition of one of the phases of **Phallic, or Sex Worship.**

PHALLIC OBJECTS, MONUMENTS AND REMAINS; Illustrations of the Rise and Development of the **Phallic Idea** (Sex Worship), and its embodiment in Works of Nature and Art. *Etched Frontispiece.*

CULTUS ARBORUM.—A Descriptive Account of **Phallic Tree Worship**, with illustrative Legends, Superstitious Usages, etc.; exhibiting its Origin and Development amongst the Eastern and Western Nations of the World, from the earliest to modern times.

This work has a valuable bibliography which will be of the greatest use and value to the student of Ancient Faiths. It contains references to nearly five hundred works on Phallism and kindred subjects.

Nature Worship and Mystical Series.—*cont.*

FISHES, FLOWERS, AND FIRE as ELEMENTS AND DEITIES in the **Phallic Faiths and Worship** of the Ancient Religions of GREECE, BABYLON, ROME, INDIA, etc., with illustrative Myths and Legends.

ARCHAIC ROCK INSCRIPTIONS; an Account of the Cup and Ring Marking on the Sculptural Stones of the Old and New Worlds. *With etched frontispiece.*

"Let any one inspect the plates in works delineating the Hindu Pantheon, and compare the drawings of the lingam-yoni with many of the rock markings we have described, with those for instance on the frontispiece of this book, and they will find it difficult to avoid the conclusion that there is a manifest and striking connection. The fact is, the phallic idea, has prevailed all over the world to a far greater extent than many have ever imagined, and superfical observers have passed by many things as inexplicable which came properly within its domain, and which thus recognised, would have been readily understood. It is not, of course, to the gross forms of the Priapus used in ancient Greek, Roman, or Egyptian Festivals that we allude, but to the much more refined, and, if we may so call it, modest lingam worship of India."—THE AUTHOR.

NATURE WORSHIP, or an Account of **Phallic Faiths** and Practices, Ancient and Modern, including the Adoration of the Male and Female Powers, and the SACTI PUJA of INDIAN GNOSTICISM, by the author of Phallicism, *with etched frontispiece.*

The subject reaches from the earliest dawn of history through long and eventful ages, down to the most modern times, and touches almost every kingdom of the past and present, in the four quarters of the earth. The unearthing of long-buried statues, monuments, and mystifying inscriptions, has suggested and provoked new lines of study among symbolical remains, and the key to so much that for long was unreadable has been found in the singular revelations of this peculiar worship.

MYSTERIES OF THE ROSIE CROSS, or the History of that Curious Sect of the Middle Ages, known as the ROSICRUCIANS, with Examples of their Pretensions and Claims.

In this work an attempt has been made to convey an intelligible idea of the peculiar mystic sect of the Rosicrucians. It is the first serious attempt to penetrate the secret recesses of this occult body, whose strange beliefs and curious practices have, ever since the days of Rosenkreutz, been enveloped in a cloud of profound mystery.

www.ingramcontent.com/pod-product-compliance
Lightning Source LLC
Chambersburg PA
CBHW030906170426
43193CB00009BA/745